OK

D0567253

WITHDRAWN

Anthony Merry *Redivivus*
A Reappraisal of
the British Minister to
the United States, 1803–6

ANTHONY MERRY, ESQ.

Painted by Gilbert Stuart at Washington in 1805. (Reproduced from a glass negative in the John Franklin Jameson Papers, courtesy of the Division of Manuscripts, Library of Congress.)

Anthony Merry *Redivivus*

A Reappraisal of
the British Minister to
the United States, 1803–6

Malcolm Lester

University Press of Virginia

Charlottesville

THE UNIVERSITY PRESS OF VIRGINIA
Copyright © 1978 by the Rector and Visitors
of the University of Virginia

First published 1978

Library of Congress Cataloging in Publication Data

Lester, Malcolm.
Anthony Merry redivivus.

Bibliography: p.
Includes Index.
1. Merry , Anthony, 1756–1835. 2. Ambassadors—
Great Britain—Biography. 3. Great Britain—
Foreign relations—United States. 4. United States
—Foreign relations—Great Britain. I. Title.
DA506.M55L47   372'.2'0924 [B]   77-20910
ISBN 0-8139-0750-0

Printed in the United States of America

To
BERNARD MAYO
Friend and Mentor

Contents

Illustrations

Preface

This monograph had its beginning nearly thirty years ago at the University of Virginia in Professor Bernard Mayo's seminar on the Age of Jefferson. Always inspiring and challenging as a seminar leader and teacher, Professor Mayo once remarked that very little was known about Anthony Merry, the third British minister to the United States. Moreover, he observed that Merry—punningly known as "Toujours Gai" to his contemporaries—was the only one of the early British ministers whose biography was not included in the *Dictionary of National Biography* and that even the dates of his birth and death seemed to be unknown. Since I was the only member of the seminar working in the field of Anglo-American relations, I suspected that Professor Mayo in his inimitable way was challenging me to write something about "Toujours Gai" Merry, for whom his winsome French poodle was named.

Some twenty years elapsed, however, before I took up the Mayo challenge. In 1966, while on sabbatical leave to do research in London on another subject, I would sometimes flee on the weekends to the English countryside from the mustiness of the Public Record Office. Because my wife and I are great admirers of John Constable's landscapes, we went one weekend to Dedham, Essex, in the heart of the country that Constable so often painted and where he spent his early years. On visiting the parish church in Dedham, I was startled to find a mural tablet to the memory of Anthony Merry, Esq., who died June 14, 1835, in his seventy-ninth year. Could this really be "Toujours Gai" Merry? Search in the Probate Registry at Somerset House in London confirmed that the Dedham Merry had indeed been the British minister to the United States. Clues in the probate records led to my finding at Guildhall Library the date of Merry's birth in the register of the extinct parish of St. Laurence Pountney. Soon after returning to Davidson, I learned that a festschrift was being planned for Professor Mayo, and I decided to write an article on Anthony Merry for that volume. It soon became apparent though that to do justice to the long-overlooked and neglected Merry, a monograph was required and not an article. Thus I trust that Professor Mayo will forgive my not being represented in his festschrift and will remember that in writing this monograph I have met his challenge of thirty years ago.

First and foremost I thank Bernard Mayo for that challenge and many others across the years. I am greatly indebted to him for reading this manuscript with the same balance of trenchant criticism and kindly encouragement that he gave seminar papers in former years. I am also indebted to Professors Dumas Malone and Julius W. Pratt for their careful reading and constructive criticism. To my colleagues Professors Charles Cornwell, Malcolm Partin, and David Shi I am grateful for their critical reading and helpful suggestions. I would also like to thank two of my former students, Professor Charles Perry of the University of the South and Professor David Jordan of Grinnell College, for taking time from their own research in London to check references for me in the Public Record Office. The Reverend Dr. Edward C. Brooks of Somerleyton, Suffolk, very kindly supplied information pertaining to Herringfleet Hall, the Merry countryseat. The Reverend Canon A. R. Johnston of Dedham, Essex, was also helpful in giving facts concerning Anthony Merry's years in Dedham. For his support I thank my senior colleague in the Department of History at Davidson College, Dr. Frontis W. Johnston, Dean of the Faculty and Chairman of the Research Committee, which generously aided this study. I gratefully acknowledge the assistance so cheerfully and efficiently given by the staff of the E. H. Little Library of Davidson College, especially the Director, Dr. Leland Park, and the Reference Librarian, Dr. Mary Beaty. To my wife I am greatly indebted for her assistance and understanding, and to my parents I am grateful for their encouragement and interest.

Davidson College   Malcolm Lester
Davidson, North Carolina
September 7, 1977

Anthony Merry *Redivivus*
A Reappraisal of
the British Minister to
the United States, 1803–6

Introduction

The years from 1803 to 1806, when Anthony Merry served as British minister to the United States, marked a turning point in the history of Anglo-American relations. During those years events and underlying forces began to disrupt the rapprochement that had been evolving since the negotiation of Jay's Treaty in 1794. The disruption had momentous consequences, for it culminated in the War of 1812. Since Merry's mission to the United States coincided with the period when the rapprochement began to break down, his role in Anglo-American diplomacy has special interest. In their account of the period, neither American nor British historians have been kind in their treatment of Merry as minister to the United States.

Henry Adams, the first American historian of prominence to treat Anglo-American relations of the early 1800s, described Merry as being "not quick of comprehension."[1] Another Harvard historian, Edward Channing, observed that he was "the least well bred and among the stupidest" of the British ministers sent to America.[2] Of Merry's residence in the United States, John Franklin Jameson, scholar par excellence of the documentary sources pertaining to Anglo-American relations of the period, said the British minister served in "pompous unhappiness."[3] The partisan Claude Bowers dubbed Merry a "pompous mediocrity."[4] Nathan Schachner, able freelance historian, contended that Merry was "as poor a diplomat as Great Britain ever sent from her shores . . . a good deal of a fool too, and easily hoodwinked."[5] Richard Beale Davis, meticulous editor of the memoirs of Merry's secretary, Augustus J. Foster, wrote that Merry was a "thin-skinned, almost stupid man already soured on everything American."[6] Bradford Perkins, somewhat less partisan in his approach than the others, considered him nevertheless "a disputatious diplomat."[7] Marshall Smelser, writing in the New American Nation series, concluded that Merry was "self important" and "a bit of a dunce."[8] Dumas Malone, the distinguished biographer of Thomas Jefferson, has most recently written that Merry was "insecure and uxorious."[9]

But if Merry's reputation has fared poorly with American historians, his fellow countrymen have seemingly concurred with those opinions by leaving blank the page in history that at least should have recorded the essential facts of his life and given some appraisal of his long career in the British diplomatic service. Of the six British ministers who served in the United States from 1791 to 1812, Anthony Merry is the only one whose biographical sketch does not appear in the *Dictionary of National Biography*. More than fifty years ago, when John Franklin Jameson discovered in London a portrait of Merry done by Gilbert Stuart, the director of the National Portrait Gallery was uninterested in obtaining that painting because Merry was not important enough to be in the DNB.[10] In his book on British ministers and ambassadors to the United States, Beckles Willson did not give the date of Merry's birth. Willson also wrote that Merry died in the West Country in 1811,[11] when he actually died in East Anglia in 1835.

Because of the inaccurate and fragmentary record of his life and the unflattering appraisals of his career, Merry should be resurrected from obscurity and reappraised in light of more recent research. Merry should be better known, for he was highly respected in his day by colleagues in the British diplomatic service. Moreover, the career of a personage accused of such ineptness in Anglo-American diplomacy ought to be reexamined.

Investigation and reappraisal of Merry are hampered by the dearth of information pertaining to his private life, especially his early years. None of his personal papers have survived, and the official correspondence of the Foreign Office in the British Public Record Office must remain the principal source for tracing his diplomatic career. Except for a few brief references in the British and American press, the only other information pertaining to Merry is found in the memoirs and private correspondence of his contemporaries. The only attempt at a full account of his diplomatic service in the United States is the chapter on Merry in Willson's *Friendly Relations*.[12] Important chapters on Merry's controversy with Thomas Jefferson and James Madison over diplomatic etiquette have been written, however, by Henry Adams, Irving Brant, and Dumas

Malone.[13] An article by Joel Larus in the *William and Mary Quarterly* on the etiquette affair and another by Anthony Steel in the *Cambridge Historical Journal* on Merry's role in the Anglo-American dispute about impressment, are the only articles pertaining to Merry that have appeared in historical journals.[14]

In the history of Anglo-American relations, the biographical dimension must always be of interest and value, despite the danger of taking the dramatis personae out of their context and thereby altering the focus of the period under study. The biographical approach to diplomatic history can contribute to historical understanding, even when there is a paucity of sources as in the case of Anthony Merry. The diplomatic historian using the biographical approach is forced to look at the past from the experience and viewpoint of one person and to thus establish, however imperfectly, personal contact with a diplomat of another era. In so doing, he adds something of a living quality to his analysis of diplomatic history, and that is one of the principal functions of the historian. The purpose of this study is to seek a deeper understanding of a significant chapter in the history of Anglo-American relations from the vantage point of a diplomat rescued in some measure from a perhaps undeserved obscurity.

I. Before the Mission to America

Anthony Merry was born August 2, 1756, in the London parish of St. Laurence Pountney.[1] His parents, Anthony and Susanna, and one sister were the only members of the immediate family. The older Merry was a City merchant engaged in the Spanish wine trade as his own father (also named Anthony) had been.[2] At one time Merry's father owned a merchant vessel, the *Lord Anson* of 600 tons burden, trading to the Mediterranean, Quebec, and Virginia. Although the father was a respected merchant and a church warden at St. Mary Abchurch, he was unsuccessful in business and was declared bankrupt in 1774.[3] Not all of the family property seems to have been lost in that year, however, for Merry presumably inherited from his father the valuable real estate that he owned in Laurence Pountney and Martin Lanes when he died in 1835.

Nothing is known of Merry's early life except that he was an exemplary and devoted son. Very likely he spent most of his youth on the premises of his father's business at 17 Laurence Pountney Lane, since City merchants in the eighteenth century usually lived in rooms above their counting houses. Laurence Pountney Lane was a dingy street sloping down towards the Thames, but nearby were such London landmarks as Fishmongers' Hall, Mansion House, and London Bridge, and such commercial centers as the Bank of England, Lloyd's Coffee House, and the Royal Exchange. Growing up in this hub of British trade, Merry—as the son of a merchant and a shipowner—was well aware from his earliest years that commerce was the lifeblood of the Empire and had to be not only pursued but also defended by diplomacy and sea power. Thus it was only natural for Merry to begin his career as an associate in business with the British consul at Malaga in Spain.[4] He entered the British foreign service in 1783 when he was named consul at Majorca in the Balearic Islands. According to his own statement, he spent nearly

all of his slender fortune in obtaining that first appointment.[5]
Merry was well qualified for the post, since he had acquired considerable knowledge of Spanish affairs from his father's wine
trade and his own experience at Malaga. This knowledge and his
proficiency in the Spanish language were assets to Merry throughout his long career in the diplomatic service.

After serving four years at Majorca, Merry became a candidate for the more important British consulate at Madrid. His
candidacy was supported by Sir Alexander Munro, the former
consul, and by Robert Liston, the British minister plenipotentiary to Spain. According to Liston, Merry had given valuable
assistance in Anglo-Spanish commercial negotiations. Moreover,
Liston declared that, of all persons in his acquaintance, Merry
was "most perfectly adapted" for the post of consul general at
Madrid. Liston lauded Merry's industry, his knowledge of commerce, especially that of Spain, and his mastery of the Spanish
language. In Liston's opinion, Merry had the character, temper,
and manners to win the affection of the Spanish people. Liston
also testified to his "gravity and reserve," characteristics distinguishing Merry during his entire career.[6]

Merry's candidacy for the Madrid post was successful, and in
June 1787, he was named consul general.[7] A highlight of his
experience in Madrid was observing in 1788 the coronation of
Charles IV as king of Spain. Despite the great expense incurred
in illuminating his house for the coronation festivities,[8] the occasion evidently meant much to Merry, for many years later he
bequeathed his coronation medals and a gold snuffbox bearing
the portrait of Charles IV to George Hammond, an old friend
whose career in the diplomatic service dated back to that period.[9] After two years as consul general in Madrid, Merry became
chargé d'affaires in the absence of a British ambassador or minister. During the time that he served as chargé, from June 1789 to
June 1790, a dispute arose between Britain and Spain over
Nootka Sound in North America. In that dispute Merry acted
with considerable ability, both while he was chargé and afterwards, when he assisted Lord St. Helens, the new British ambassador who arrived in June 1790.[10]

In January 1790, Merry sent to the British Foreign Office the

first report of what had happened the year before at Nootka
Sound, in what is now called Vancouver Island in British Columbia. In 1789, Spanish warships had forestalled a British attempt
to establish a settlement on Nootka Sound by seizing the British
post and trading vessels. Merry continued to send other important details concerning the incident and accounts of his interviews with Floridablanca, the Spanish minister. His reports were
accurate, and his interpretation of events and possible developments was sound. Merry was warned by the Duke of Leeds, the
British foreign secretary, to be extremely guarded in his dealings
with Spanish officials, and there is no intimation that he departed
from these instructions. Merry reported that, despite the warlike
preparations being made in Spain, the Spanish did not really
seek war with Britain, and in view of subsequent developments,
he was correct. [11]

In May 1789, the British foreign secretary had decided to send
as ambassador to Spain, Lord St. Helens, an accomplished
diplomatist. When the ambassador arrived, he relied greatly on
Merry's assistance and judgment. This association was the beginning of a long friendship remembered by Merry in his will. [12]
After concluding a settlement with Spain, Lord St. Helens
declared that he needed no embassy secretary because Merry was
an admirable assistant "whose talents for business and other
merits" could not be praised too highly. [13] Indeed, Merry's forte
for detail and correctness of protocol made him particularly useful in Spain, where the punctilio of the Spanish court probably
intensified his zeal.

Merry remained in Madrid as consul general until late 1796,
when Spain declared war against Britain after concluding an
alliance with France. [14] Apparently he was unemployed during
1797 and 1798, but in April 1799, he became consul general to
Denmark, Prussia, and Sweden, with his consulate at Copenhagen. In the absence of a British ambassador to Denmark, he
served from July 1799 to September 1800, as chargé d'affaires for
a second time in his career. [15] Life was not as pleasant for Merry in
Copenhagen as it had been in Spain. He complained about his
miserable lodgings and the "insufferable" style of society. An
astute English observer, however, thought that Merry overstated

his difficulties and made himself somewhat ridiculous by running up and down and asking the Danish merchants, "Why don't you join our coalition?" Merry, according to the same observer, was too inclined to view the literary men of Copenhagen as being "great Jacobins."[16]

The next assignment for Merry was distinctly diplomatic rather than consular. In October 1801, he was named secretary to the British embassy headed by Lord Cornwallis that was sent to Amiens to negotiate a definitive treaty of peace with France.[17] Joseph Bonaparte, Napoleon's younger brother, represented the French. Shortly after the negotiations began in December, Cornwallis wrote an aide that while Merry was efficient in business and had many good qualities, he did not "conduce much to amusement" of the embassy. Moreover, Cornwallis, as Joseph Bonaparte recalled years later, said that Merry was "a little Portuguese, not an Englishman," a probable reference to Merry's diminutive size and his long residence in the Iberian region.[18]

But despite Merry's drabness and meticulousness, he was of invaluable help to the diplomatically inexperienced Cornwallis. From the beginning of the Amiens negotiations, Cornwallis was reported as being uncomfortable in the diplomatic arena, where he had expected to have an easy time.[19] Rumor in diplomatic circles had it that because of the "drowsiness" of Cornwallis, Merry wrote all of the dispatches. Though Merry thought well and was "strongheaded," he was unable to cope with Joseph Bonaparte, who was cleverly prompted from Paris by Talleyrand.[20] In these circumstances it was not surprising that Cornwallis departed from Amiens as soon as possible and left Merry to conclude the negotiations.[21]

By the time of his departure, however, Lord Cornwallis had come to have a high regard for Merry and handsomely acknowledged his role in the Amiens negotiations. He recommended Merry to the favorable attention of the ministry and declared that he had placed great reliance on his experience and correctness. His lordship also commended Merry for his talents and assiduity.[22] Merry, however, did not have an equal regard for Cornwallis and his role in the negotiations. He confided to a friend that he was worn out with "moral and physical fatigue" resulting from the long night sessions and the preparation of documents, with stretches sometimes of twenty-four hours of incessant writing. All of this work he resented, for it arose from the total incapacity of Cornwallis, the "Old Woman," with whom he had been so unfortunately associated. Joseph Bonaparte, according to Merry, often looked at him and smiled at the incompetence of Cornwallis. Although Merry may have sought to appear as an astute and overworked subordinate and therefore exaggerated his difficulties at Amiens, he was being realistic when he lamented that he expected to receive no credit in England for his labors, since the definitive treaty would be regarded as worse than the preliminaries signed earlier. [23]

Following the conclusion of negotiations and the signing of the Treaty of Amiens on March 27, 1802, Merry was named Birtish minister ad interim at Paris. In that post he succeeded his old friend Francis James Jackson, with whom he had been associated in Spain from 1791 to 1795. On April 18 Merry presented his credentials to Napoleon and soon thereafter exchanged the ratifications of the Treaty of Amiens as his first official business. [24] Until his recall in September, Merry was vigilant in observing Napoleon's aggressive moves. Among those moves that he reported to the Foreign Office were the equipping of a fleet at Toulon as well as Napoleon's plans for the dismemberment of the Turkish Empire and the acquisition of a port in the Mediterranean that was nearer to Egypt. In view of these ominous developments, the British government decided in September to replace Merry with a diplomat of higher rank, and Lord Whitworth was sent to France in the fall of 1802. [25]

Merry estimated that during his service in Paris from April to September, he wrote almost without any assistance 130 public and private letters to the Foreign Office and about 50 letters to Talleyrand and that he handled some 2,100 passports, his most trying work. Added to all this were altercations, applications, notes, and recommendations involving 3,000 visiting Englishmen, many of whom were determined to get a glimpse of Napoleon. But even though overwhelmed by paper work, Merry sought to oblige the numerous visitors coming to Paris from England. In that procession was the writer Madame d'Arblay, née

Fanny Burney, who testified to Merry's kindness in 1802. Because of her friendship with the royal family, Merry hastened to proffer his services to Madame d'Arblay, and he must have been pleased to note that several of her many letters sent to England in his diplomatic pouch were directed to Queen Charlotte and the royal princesses.[26]

Merry was vexed and apprehensive when he heard that, despite all the efforts he had made to satisfy his fellow countrymen, he was to be castigated in the English newspapers for the way he had performed his duties. He was criticized for his failure to give a dinner in honor of the birthday of George III on June 4, even though his modest stipend did not permit such a lavish outlay. More ominous for his future in the diplomatic service was the unintentional offense he gave two visiting leaders of the Whig opposition. Among the British visitors to Paris in the summer of 1802 were Charles James Fox and Thomas Erskine. The latter, a distinguished barrister notorious for his egotism and vanity, became particularly annoyed with the British minister.[27] Merry, fatigued by making numerous presentations, introduced Erskine to Napoleon, not by name, but by his official title of chancellor to the Prince of Wales. Because of this incomplete introduction, Napoleon paid little attention to Erskine and only indifferently asked him if he were a lawyer. Erskine's pique was accentuated when the First Consul in a later interview alluded to Merry's introduction and said to the distinguished visitor, "You are better known to me by your name than your office."[28] The marked attention paid these "opposition people" from England by Napoleon and Talleyrand caused Merry much trouble and uneasiness. No wonder he considered all of this "horrible and indecent" and wished to be relieved from his disagreeable and anxious situation.[29]

Among those seeking passport validation from Merry in order to visit England were two Americans, Joel Barlow and Robert Fulton. Grave Merry might have been indulging in a bit of humor when he reminded British officials of Fulton's submarine experiments in the Seine and wrote the Latin phrase *verbum sapientibus*, "a word to the wise," on the communication.[30] Merry, however, was not alone in playing with words and phrases, for none other than Napoleon made

a punning and satirical reference to Merry's name, the motto "toujours gai" inscribed on Merry's personal seal, and the sobriquet by
which he was known to friends in the diplomatic service. Dour
Merry was jestingly dubbed *Monsieur Toujours Rire* by the First Consul, who, nevertheless, presented him with a gold snuffbox as a token
of his esteem.[31]

"Toujours Gai," despite his onerous diplomatic duties, might well
have smiled more during the summer of 1802 than he was ordinarily
wont to do, for in Paris that summer he met and courted his future
wife. Visiting Paris in 1802 was the widow of John Leathes, Esq.,
of Herringfleet Hall in Suffolk. According to an unsubstantiated
tradition, Mrs. Leathes, née Elizabeth Death, was the daughter of a
farmer in Herringfleet parish. Marriage to Squire Leathes was thus
above her station, and in the opinion of some, that accounted for her
hauteur.[32] But although her pedigree cannot be determined with
certainty, the lady was known to many as a charming hostess and a
good conversationalist, with a scholarly interest in botany.[33] Her
portrait painted in America by Gilbert Stuart in 1805 reveals a
striking and handsome woman.[34] Augustus J. Foster, grandson
of the Earl of Bristol and stepson of the Duke of Devonshire, considered her a "fine woman," as did Thomas Moore, the Irish poet.[35]

Mrs. Leathes included in her circle of friends Lady Cecilia
Johnston, daughter of the Earl De La Warr and wife of Lieutenant
General James Johnston, and Lady Mary DeBeede, a member of the
Princess of Orange's family.[36] The prominent Leathes family of
Suffolk belonged to the gentry and obviously accepted Elizabeth
Death without qualm. Years later, her second husband bequeathed
the Gilbert Stuart portrait to John Francis Leathes, a favorite
nephew by marriage, who inherited Herringfleet Hall at her
death.[37] After the death of John Leathes in 1788, Mrs. Leathes had
presided alone over Herringfleet Hall since there were no children.
Perhaps growing weary of her rustication in Suffolk, she sought diversion in France along with other Britons following the Peace of
Amiens.

The circumstances in which the widow Leathes made the acquaintance of Anthony Merry are unknown. Merry, however, in 1802 was
in the mood to consider matrimony seriously. Moreover, the forty-
six-year-old bachelor was being spurred on by the advice of a friend.

ELIZABETH MERRY

Painted by Gilbert Stuart at Washington in 1805. (Reproduced from Lawrence Park's *Gilbert Stuart* [1926], 4:330, courtesy of William E. Rudge Sons Division of Harwyn Industries Corporation.)

The arrival of a charming widow on the scene about that time provided another spur. Although Merry was attracted to the lady, he did not overlook such a practical matter as the widow's fortune. While it consisted of only a jointure for her lifetime, he considered that it would give significant "assistance" to his income. The practical Merry also noted that since the widow had had no children by her first marriage, it was unlikely that there would be any burden "of that kind" for him. Aware in 1802 of the possibility of a diplomatic assignment to America and perhaps also to Spain, Merry recognized that his courtship would have to be vigorously pursued, because time was short. He lamented that his busy schedule did not allow the leisure "to lay siege to a Fortress, the more difficult to approach as having been strengthened by years of the knowledge and enjoyment of its independence."[38]

Despite his interest in Mrs. Leathes, Merry was not unmindful of other matrimonial possibilities. When an acquaintance suggested that he also consider the daughter of Sir Philip Stephens, former secretary of the Admiralty and member of Parliament, he asked a friend to get a view of her and send him his opinion. In the meantime he expected to continue "dabbling about" the widow Leathes. According to his investigation, the lady had excellent sense, a good disposition, and (not least in importance), a good income for life. Unfortunately, though, she did not enjoy good health and was not eager to cross the Atlantic if Merry should be sent to America. Both Merry and Mrs. Leathes were aware by the early fall of 1802 that rumor linked their names romantically and had it that they were to be married. The prudent Merry, however, was still uncertain about the extent of the Leathes estate and asked his confidant Francis James Jackson to see what he could find out in England concerning it.[39] Apparently Merry satisfied himself on all points and was able to breach successfully the walls of the "fortress," since he and Mrs. Leathes were married in the London home of Lady Cecilia Johnston on January 21, 1803.[40]

II.   Minister to the United States

Eight days after his marriage, Merry was gazetted on January 29, 1803, to be His Britannic Majesty's envoy extraordinary and minister plenipotentiary to the United States.[1] The possibility of his appointment was first mentioned by an American official in September 1800, about the time that Merry returned to England from his service at Copenhagen. Rufus King, then the American minister to England, advised the State Department in that month that Merry would probably succeed Robert Liston as British minister to the United States. Although he reported that Merry appeared to have a favorable record, King said that he would make a more thorough investigation of his qualifications.[2] While King's investigation was proceeding, the foreign secretary, Lord Grenville, announced to King that Merry would be sent to the United States and expressed confidence that the Americans would find him most acceptable.[3]

Merry, however, did not receive his credentials in 1800 as minister to the United States. The Foreign Office presumably decided that his services were needed elsewhere, and in 1801 he was appointed secretary to the British embassy that negotiated the Peace of Amiens. While Merry was in France, Lord Hawkesbury, Grenville's successor at the Foreign Office, informed Rufus King that Merry's friend, Francis James Jackson, would be sent to America instead of Merry. King in the meantime had become acquainted with both Jackson and Merry and regretted the change. Jackson he considered vain, intolerant, and unfriendly to the United States. In view of Jackson's unsatisfactory record as British minister to the United States in 1809, King's evaluation was correct. On the other hand, King found Anthony Merry to be a "plain, unassuming, sensible man."[4] It is interesting that King's description of Merry was almost identical with that by Lord Malmesbury, the distinguished diplomatist, who described him as a "sensible, plain man."[5] According to King, Jackson was ambitious and eager for immediate appointment and would leave America whenever a preferable post became available, but Merry sought only "an agreeable and permanent residence." Rufus King tactfully persuaded Hawkesbury, as a friendly act to the United States, to reconsider and send Merry instead of Jackson. The foreign secretary, however, told King that Merry must first complete his assignment in France and perhaps even go to Madrid before going to America.[6] Although Merry was eventually sent to the United States, the Foreign Office apparently did not inform Merry of the promise made the American minister, for Merry was wondering in September of 1802 whether he was still slated to take the American assignment that had been pending for more than two years.[7]

Following his return to England in the fall of 1802, Merry was occupied with plans for his approaching marriage to Mrs. Leathes in January 1803. He was also engaged in making preparations for the voyage to America, since by October 8 he had at last been apprised of his appointment to the American mission.[8] Merry, however, did not expect to leave for America before February 1803. Preparations apparently took longer than Merry had anticipated, for in March Rufus King reported that the Foreign Office was urging Merry to be ready for departure during the first week in April.[9]

Although the American minister was pleased with Merry's appointment, one outspoken Englishman and advocate of friendly relations with the United States received the news with great displeasure. William Cobbett, the radical editor, criticized the appointment on the grounds that Merry was too obscure a person for a post so important to Anglo-American relations. Despite Cobbett's denunciation of the Amiens treaty as the work of "peddling politicians" and "grovelling statesmen," he was apparently not critical of Merry either on the grounds of personal acquaintance or because of his part in the Amiens negotiations.[10] Indeed, Merry would have agreed with Cobbett that the terms of the definitive treaty were unsatisfactory.

"Who is Mr. Merry?" Cobbett asked disparagingly and then proceeded to compare him unfavorably with such prominent Americans as John Adams, Thomas Pinckney, and Rufus King, all of whom had represented the United States at the Court of St. James's. Cobbett wondered whether it was a decorous or just policy for Britain to reciprocate by sending as ministers to the United States former consuls, chargés d'affaires, and secretaries, "the mere stop-gaps and journeymen of the corps diplomatic, men who have been trained up to the trade, who follow diplomacy for bread, who (to pass over their incapacity) have not the means to give a dinner, and if they had, have not the manners to receive and entertain their guests." According to Cobbett, such a person would hardly be fit to represent Britain in a country with which she had a greater and closer connection than with any other upon earth, especially a country that was at so great a distance from London that instructions in emergencies were impossible to send and the British minister had to act on his own.

The only reason that Cobbett could discern for the appointment of Merry was the desire of Downing Street and the Treasury to provide for him on account of his past services. If this were the reason, the editor urged, "let him be provided for, give him a pension, give him a sinecure . . . but in God's name let him not go to the country in which, above all others, we stand in need of a great, enlightened, and high-minded statesman."[11] Two weeks after this outburst Cobbett returned to the attack on Merry's appointment when rumor reached London that General Bernadotte was being sent to the United States as French minister. Although Bernadotte did not go, Cobbett sarcastically commented on what a "noble figure" that "poor Mr. Merry" would make by the side of the general, who would "ride over him . . . tread him in the dust," and probably drive him from Washington. Merry would not be needed in the American capital anyway, sneered Cobbett, for there would be no passports to countersign and no visiting English nobility for him to serve as gentleman usher.[12]

While Cobbett may have been very nearly correct in his appraisal of Merry's qualifications and perhaps even wise in his recommendation that a "great, enlightened, and high-minded statesman" should be sent to America, it is unlikely that such a person would have accepted the appointment if he had been available or if the British government had been inclined to proffer it. Under the circumstances,—the validity of Cobbett's criticism notwithstanding,—Merry, because of his age, his experience, and the nature of his recent assignments, appeared to be a suitable candidate for the American post. Moreover, it should not be overlooked that Rufus King, an astute judge of the qualifications required, approved of Merry.

Cobbett's diatribes against Merry's appointment went unheeded: with the appointment already sanctioned by the American minister in advance of the official announcement in the *London Gazette,* matters had gone too far for the government to consider a revocation even if it had been so disposed. It is possible, however, that Cobbett's criticisim caused Merry to seek out Rufus King, the retiring American minister, and James Monroe, successor to King, and to confer with them concerning Anglo-American affairs.[13] These conversations were made possible because the resumption of war in May 1803 between Britain and France presumably delayed Merry's departure until September. He must have gleaned some insight into the state of Anglo-American relations when he was a guest at a dinner given by the Duke of Portland shortly before King left London in May. His fellow guests included King; Henry Addington, the prime minister; Lord Hawkesbury, the foreign secretary; and Merry's old friend George Hammond, who was under-secretary at the Foreign Office and a former minister to the United States.[14] During the summer of 1803 Merry had several conversations with James Monroe, the new American minister. Merry favorably impressed Monroe, who described the Englishman as being a man of "candour and good views."[15]

Ten days after Monroe wrote this favorable evaluation, Merry and his suite sailed from Portsmouth on September 28, 1803, aboard the frigate *Phaeton.*[16] Arriving at Norfolk on November 4 after a long and tedious voyage, Merry,—ever observant of diplomatic protocol,—on that same day notified the American secretary of state of his arrival.[17] Unfortunately Merry could not proceed directly to Washington because overland transportation was unavailable, and he and Mrs. Merry were compelled to remain at Norfolk as the guests of Col. John Hamilton, the British consul. Not only was their arrival in America marred by this delay, but Mrs. Merry developed a fever after being attacked by Norfolk mosquitoes.[18] When a vessel was finally obtained to carry them up the Chesapeake and the Potomac to the capital city, gales and contrary winds, with which their ignorant navigators could not cope, slowed their progress, and they did not arrive at Alexandria until November 25, after a voyage of six days from Norfolk.[19] Thomas Moore, the young Irish poet, had crossed the Atlantic with the Merrys on his way to become registrar of the vice-admiralty court at Bermuda, and to him Mrs. Merry sent a description of the country as seen from aboard ship. She commented on the awe-inspiring "immensity" of the landscape, but she also mentioned the sameness of the scenery, lack of cultivation and barrenness of the hills and trees in November. She also noted the "miserable" huts of the Negroes and the unsanitary conditions that caused disease to be rife in the country.[20]

At Alexandria the Merrys were met by Edward Thornton, secretary of the British legation and chargé d'affaires since the departure of Robert Liston, the last British minister, in 1800. Thornton escorted them to Georgetown in the District of Columbia by "coachie," a primitive type of carriage. According to Mrs. Merry, the roads were intolerable and the cold severe. But despite her discomfort, she was amused by the "inward groanings" of her husband as the coachie jolted and swayed. At their destination the Merrys were unable to obtain the house that they had expected to occupy and were forced to put up at a Georgetown inn. Here Mrs. Merry made her first acquaintance with the typical American innkeeper of the times, who breezily informed her that he kept no schedule whatever for serving meals but that she could have her dinner,—a meal so bad that neither Mistress Merry nor His Britannic Majesty's minister could eat a morsel of it. No wonder that poor Mr. Merry groaned that America was a thousand times worse than the worst parts of Spain.[21] From the inelegant surroundings of this Georgetown inn, Merry apprised James Madison of his arrival in the federal district and asked when he might call and be presented to him and the president.[22]

For her part, Mrs. Merry at first resolved to bear up bravely and good humoredly under the situation. She was amused by the stir caused among Americans by the quantity of the new minister's luggage. It seems that the Americans could not imagine why so much was needed and speculated that the British minister was slipping in British goods to sell without paying duty. Likewise, the entourage of servants accompanying the Merrys created a stir. The staff must have seemed enormous to the Americans, for in Merry's note to the State Department concerning his establishment, he listed in addition to Secretary Thornton: a Piedmontese maître d'hôtel, a French cook, an English valet de chambre, a Swiss footman, an Irish servant to Thornton, an English coachman, an English groom, a Scots maid for Mrs. Merry, an English housemaid, an American Negro helper in the kitchen, and three Negro women in the laundry and scullery.[23] Surely this was a ménage extensive and cosmopolitan for the rural and democratic surroundings of the American capital in 1803.

About the time that the Merry retinue was getting settled in Washington, Rufus King, whom Merry had consulted in England respecting "domestic matters at that place," expressed the hope that Merry would find himself tolerably comfortable, for otherwise the tone of his reports back to London might be influenced by his difficulties. King was remarkably prescient, for Merry's first weeks in America were extremely trying because of living conditions and did lead to unflattering reports regarding his situation.[24] On the same day that King expressed his concern, Merry wrote George Hammond that living conditions in Washington were "perfectly savage." He reported that he had succeeded with great difficulty and expense in renting two houses or rather two "mere shells" thrown together. The houses had no fixtures, not even a pump or a well. Not only did Merry find housing inadequate and expensive, but provisions, especially vegetables, were dear and difficult to obtain at any price; some items had to be brought from Baltimore, and butter even had to come from Philadelphia. Merry wailed that "the difficulties and misery in every respect" of his situation could hardly be described.[25]

To assist with the difficulties of getting settled, Merry did have the capable help of Edward Thornton. Although Thornton had received permission to return to England when Merry arrived, he obligingly stayed on until July 1804.[26] After his departure, the Merrys must have missed him sorely, for Augustus J. Foster, his successor, did not reach Washington until December. The Merrys were grateful for the "indefatigable efforts" of Thornton, a quiet, sensible, and well-informed Englishman who strove to procure every possible comfort for them.[27] What the slow-talking but astute Thornton (who subsequently had a distinguished diplomatic career) thought of the Merrys was not revealed, but Anthony Merry hardly had the qualifications that Thornton had earlier said a British minister to the United States should have. Thornton had advised Lord Hawkesbury that the British interest in America called for a minister of high rank, distinguished by title as well as by station in society. A diplomat with the assurance of such a background would not be afraid to debase himself as he moved in a society where the manners of gentlemen did not always prevail. Thornton also suggested that the British minister should be surrounded with opulence and splendor in order to provide lavish hospitality needed in the American capital which was so lacking in amenities.[28]

Thornton probably recognized that any British minister who followed the able, friendly, and imaginative Robert Liston, Merry's friend since his Spanish days, would have a difficult time. Alexander Baring, another Englishman familiar with the American scene, expressed the view that Liston's successor would find it no easy task to make himself agreeable to the Americans whatever his qualifications might be.[29]

The warnings and forebodings of Thornton and Baring should have been heeded in England, because a British minister to republican and democratic America under Thomas Jefferson needed adaptability and flexibility, patience and tact, to an uncommon degree. Anthony Merry was certainly not the non-entity that caustic William Cobbett made him out to be, for he had talent, experience, and the good opinion both of colleagues in the British diplomatic service and of respected American representatives abroad such as Rufus King, Christopher Gore, and James Monroe.

But despite favorable views of Merry, there were significant clues in the comments of Englishmen who admired and respected him to indicate that he was an unfortunate choice for the American post. Moreover, his wife, despite her charm and cultural attainments, was an unfortunate companion for a husband with an American assignment. Henry Adams described Merry as being a "thorough Englishman, with a wife more English than himself.[30] This was true, but his predecessor, the Scotsman Robert Liston, was a thorough Briton, as was his wife Henrietta—though, because of her colonial origin in Antigua, she might have had more insight into provincial American ways than did Elizabeth Merry. More important in appraising Merry's suitability for the American post than his Englishry were his temperament and the nature of his diplomatic experience. Being extremely precise and correct might have made for success in Europe but did not necessarily qualify him for an American assignment. The appointment of the inapt Merry was ironical, for aspiring young diplomats like Augustus J. Foster— whose uncle Lord Hawkesbury, the foreign secretary, advised him to become a member of Merry's mission—considered it a privilege to serve under him because of his talents and his knowledge of diplomatic procedure. Even after Merry had been recalled, Foster lamented that he would be deprived of his valuable instruction.[31]

It is significant, however, that Foster, who respected Merry and appreciated his kindness, also smiled at "Toujours Gai" and the meticulous ways that in large measure accounted for much of his difficulty and lack of success in America. Foster recognized that Merry had a tenacious memory of everything said to him, was observant of everything, had a wide acquaintance of people in Europe that made his conversations about persons and characters inexhaustible, but that he was decidedly lacking in imagination. According to Foster, he was full of honor and integrity: indeed, Foster thought there was never a "worthier man." Foster also recognized that Merry was "slow, methodical, strictly *en règle*, indefatigable, clearsighted and vigilant," and perhaps most revealingly, that Merry carried on his duties "like clockwork."[32] Another secretary in later years remembered him as "the gentlest of plenipotentiaries."[33] Senator William Plumer of New Hampshire observed that though Merry had "considerable knowledge of man and the forms of business" and was "easy, polite, and very civil," he was "neither the scholar nor man of talents."[34]

Caution was another distinguishing trait of Merry the diplomat. George Jackson, brother of Francis James Jackson, once stated that Merry was a "most cautious man," and James Madison described him as "excessively cautious."[35] On the eve of the War of 1812, Thomas Jefferson alluded to the caution of "poor Merry," who had "learned nothing of diplomacy but suspicions without head enough to distinguish when they were misplaced."[36] Merry's cautious nature is also illustrated by a story attributed to John Randolph of Roanoke, who said that when Merry was asked "what o'clock is it?" he would be apt to reply, "I will write to my government for instructions."[37]

Excessive caution coupled with the temperament of a clockwork minister did not augur well for Merry in the United States, where he would have to deal with the new and the unexpected. Moreover, Merry was handicapped while in America by either bad health or hypochondria, or perhaps a combination of both. Foster, soon after becoming Merry's secretary, wrote that Merry was in perpetual alarm "lest his disorder should return."[38] This disorder, for which Merry had to undergo surgery at Philadelphia in the fall of 1804, was hemorrhoids, an ailment not only painful but nerve-racking.[39] Ill health continued to plague Merry, and just before he left America in 1806, Foster observed that the poor man was a "martyr to ill health" and bore it "like a woman."[40] The impression of a complaining, fussy, censorious man emerges. In addition there was extreme sensitivity and anxiety on Merry's part that the dignity of his position be recognized at all times. Not having been born to a privileged station in life, he found it difficult, as Edward Thornton feared such a minister might, to accommodate himself to democratic ways by overlooking slights, intentional or unintentional.

Merry, though, did make a favorable initial impression in America. A month after his arrival and even after irritations had arisen, James Madison reported that he appeared to be "an amicable man in private society and a candid and agreeable one in public business," and seven months later Madison declared, "He is at bottom a very worthy man and easy to do business with except that he is excessively cautious."[41] None other than President Jefferson concluded that Merry was "personally as desirable a character as could have been sent." To Jefferson he appeared to be such "a reasonable and good man" that the American government would be sorry to lose him. [42] The Reverend Manasseh Cutler, a Federalist congressman and a fair-minded observer, found Merry to be a "well-informed and genteel man, extremely easy and social." [43] On the other hand, Margaret Bayard Smith, wife of the editor of the *National Intelligencer,* the administration newspaper in Washington, said he was plain in appearance and was considered rather inferior in understanding and that he passed quite unnoticed in company with his wife, who was "so entirely the talker and actor." [44] Perhaps another reason Merry tenaciously sought to uphold the dignity of his official position was that he had to assert himself in order to bolster his ego and to maintain the respect of his wife.

Impressions of Mrs. Merry, both favorable and unfavorable, were more pronounced than those of her husband. Jefferson, though he had a favorable view of Merry at first, thought that the minister was "unluckily associated" with a "virago" of a wife who had disturbed the harmony of Washington society. [45] Mrs. Smith described Mrs. Merry as "a tall, well-made woman, rather masculine, but easy without being graceful" and who was said to have "a fine under-standing." [46] If Mrs. Merry fared poorly in the estimation of President Jefferson, Vice-President Aaron Burr, no mean judge of womanflesh, wrote that she was tall, fair, and pleasantly plump, with grace, dignity, sprightfulness, and intelligence, a woman who had lived in Paris and who had all that could be wished of the manners of both France and England. She was such an amicable and interesting person that Burr expressed a desire for his daughter Theodosia to make her acquaintance. [47] The Reverend Mr. Cutler was as complimentary of Mrs. Merry as he was of her husband. He thought that she was a "remarkable fine woman" who "entered instantly into the most agreeable conversation." [48] Cutler's good opinion of Mrs. Merry increased, especially when he learned that, like himself, she was an enthusiastic botanist and was interested in collecting specimens of American plants. Mrs. Merry presented Cutler with botanical books and also her picture just before she returned to England and promised to send the clergyman seeds from the botanical garden of Cambridge University. [49] Cutler noted that Mrs. Merry was particularly critical of the dreary, uncultivated country around Washington and the lack of taste in gardens and walks. She also criticized the failure of American women to decorate their rooms with flowers and their tendency to read only "foolish novels."[50]

These favorable opinions of Mrs. Merry's attainments and talents by her admirers were, as in the case of her husband, tempered by a recognition of certain faults that foreshadowed difficulty in her role as the wife of a diplomat to the United States. Augustus J. Foster admitted that she was accustomed to adulation and at times was overbearing, that she lived on conversation and probably never would have looked in a book if she had anybody with whom to talk.[51] In writing to his mother about a friend who had married beneath his station, Thomas Moore added significantly and with awe, "Oh if Mrs. Merry were to know that!"[52] George Jackson commented that she was restless and thrived on being puffed up by the position of her husband.[53] While these observations are significant, they do not necessarily suggest that Mrs. Merry's hauteur was compensation for not being to the manner born. The lady had been accepted for too many years by the English gentry and aristocracy for that to be the only explanation.

The record of Mrs. Merry's own comments about America reveals to a great extent a condescending and patronizing attitude. In her first letter to Thomas Moore after reaching Washington, she wrote about living in a hovel and exhibiting herself at the Capitol, which she said was a profanation of the term, and she sneered at the name Tiber River given to a "dirty arm" of the Potomac.[54] Perhaps the new American Capitol was a profanation in its unfinished state, but imagination and sympathetic insight would have presented a more magnanimous view of the new Federal city. But the best Elizabeth Merry could do was to sigh for the patience that she said was needed to deal with the "ignorance and self conceit" of the Americans.[55] The image of an imperious, garrulous, supercilious woman emerges—a woman who had many accomplishments, but not those that would have been helpful for the wife of a British minister to the United States in 1803.

The temperament and background of the new minister and his lady inevitably influenced the conduct of diplomacy during their triennium in America. But before Merry's effectiveness as a diplomat can be examined and appraised, the general state of Anglo-

American relations in 1803, at the beginning of his mission, must be considered. On the same day that Merry arrived in Washington, a proadministration newspaper, the *Aurora* of Philadelphia, declared that the new British minister arrived at a time never "more favorable to amiable and generous views" in Anglo-American relations.[56] While some Americans might fear a renewal of bad feelings promoted in certain instances by Merry's predecessors and some might even hope to embroil the United States in foreign difficulties, the *Aurora* recognized that many believed Britain sincerely wanted friendship with America.

A new minister ordinarily would have been heartened by such a pronouncement, but the clipping containing the statement—which Merry sent to the Foreign Office along with the observation that the *Aurora* was under government direction—went in a dispatch that also contained an account of an affront that he and his wife had received at the President's House. Merry may very well have thought that the *Aurora* had been overly amiable and generous in its assessment of Anglo-American relations.

Yet a note similarly optimistic to that of the *Aurora* had been sounded earlier in the year by the British chargé d'affaires in Washington. Edward Thornton in January testified that he had witnessed a great change in the attitude of the Jefferson administration and that even a spirit of cordial cooperation seemed to prevail, though at the same time he noted a tendency of Secretary of State James Madison's to be less than frank.[57] President Jefferson had gone so far as to say that Britain was a bulwark against France,[58] and in the previous year, when the president feared that the French might occupy New Orleans, he had even mentioned a possible marriage of his country to the British fleet and nation.[59] The peace in Europe that extended from the treaty of Amiens to the resumption of war in May of 1803 had ended for the time being the maritime disputes that had bedeviled Anglo-American relations for so long.

In Britain a conciliatory ministry with Henry Addington as prime minister and Lord Hawkesbury as foreign secretary facilitated the signing of two Anglo-American conventions that, it seemed, might remove any remaining difficulties. The first convention, negotiated in 1802, reactivated the debt and spoliation commissions established by Jay's Treaty in 1794, but which had been suspended for five years. The second convention, however, was not ratified, because the British in 1804 declined to accept the American deletion of the provision pertaining to the Northwest boundary. Moreover, the efforts of Rufus King to persuade the British in 1803 to outlaw impressment on the high seas came to naught.

These last failures were directly related to two events in the spring of 1803 that would soon affect Anglo-American harmony, even though at the end of that year the *Aurora* still considered an optimistic view to be justified. The first event was the purchase of Louisiana on April 30, 1803, which enabled the United States to take a more independent stand vis-à-vis Great Britain. The Louisiana Purchase also led in 1804 to the deletion of the article in the 1803 convention delineating the boundary in the Northwest as being along a direct line from the northwesternmost corner of the Lake of the Woods to the source of the Mississippi River, for fear that the boundaries of the Louisiana Purchase might be compromised in some way. The second event, the declaration of war between Britain and France on May 15, 1803, caused the British Admiralty to defeat Rufus King's proposal against impressment, because of an anticipated shortage of seamen. The resumption of war was also followed by the inevitable Anglo-American recriminations over neutral and belligerent rights and obligations in maritime affairs.

These difficulties began to arise even before James Monroe, Rufus King's successor, arrived in London and also before Anthony Merry had left England. When word reached America that Britain and France were again at war, Thornton and Madison began to discuss the old problems such as the presence of French privateers in American ports, the use of American waters as operating stations by British cruisers, and the impressment of American seamen. After bluntly warning Thornton that the United States would not permit the same infringement of her neutral rights that had been suffered in the previous war,[60] Madison stated categorically that the American government did not recognize the legality of impressment.[61]

In view of the acrimonious discussion with Madison, Thornton was worried that there might be a serious deterioration in Anglo-American relations before the new minister arrived. He lamented that appearance of a "bitterness of tone" in Madison's commuications—that resembled too much the "character of the public papers"—and he deplored the taking of positions contravening the recognized authorities in international law. Yet Thornton did not believe that President Jefferson, with whom he was able to talk more easily, would have approved either Madison's language or his interpretation.[62]

Thornton's account of these discussions had not reached England when Merry's instructions were prepared in September. Even if they had included Thornton's latest advice, those instructions were woefully inadequate for a new British minister going to the United States, particularly at a time when the international situation was fraught with such momentous consequences for Anglo-American relations. Hawkesbury, from the tenor of his instructions to Merry, assumed that all points in dispute between Britain and America had been settled by Jay's Treaty and the conventions of 1802 and 1803.

Merry was enjoined in the most conventional terms to promote and improve the harmony "so happily" existing between the two countries and to cultivate a good understanding with the American officials. Completely ignoring the potentially explosive issue of impressments and American trade with enemy colonies, Hawkesbury gave no guidance whatever on maritime affairs, with the exception of reminding Merry that he should urge the Americans to prevent the fitting out and succoring of enemy privateers in their ports, which should also be closed to enemy prizes whenever they consisted of British vessels and goods. Hawkesbury's instructions dealt with such routine matters as the transfer of money awarded Britain by the commissioners appointed under Jay's Treaty and the appointment of commissioners provided for under the boundary convention of 1803. According to the instructions he gave Merry, Hawkesbury apparently thought that the most pressing point for his first discussions with the American government was the seeking of a disclaimer of the sentiments expressed by Robert Livingston, the American minister to France, to the effect that France and the United

States had a common interest in opposing Britain's "maritime tyranny."[63]

In some measure the omissions in Hawkesbury's instructions were supplied by none other than the American representatives in London. Shortly before Merry sailed in September, James Monroe discussed with him the problems of impressment and interference with American commerce by the British.[64] In their discussions Merry carefully noted these matters, and when he later told Monroe that he had conferred with Lord Hawkesbury concerning them, the American minister concluded that was a good indication for thinking the new minister would do well in his assignment to the United States. The failure of the Foreign Office to give any guidance to Merry concerning American trade to the enemy colony of St. Domingue so alarmed Christopher Gore,—an American commissioner to the Joint Spoliations Commission established under Jay's Treaty and the Federalist chargé d'affaires before the arrival of Monroe,—that he urged Merry to confer specifically on this point with Lord Hawkesbury, who, even then, did not give any directions in the matter.[65]

While Merry was crossing the Atlantic with such inadequate instructions, Edward Thornton in America was increasingly apprehensive about the state of Anglo-American affairs. He was especially concerned that the stipulations of Jay's Treaty closing American ports to French privateers would soon expire, a point that Hawkesbury had evidently overlooked.[66] Thornton was also disturbed by a complaint from Madison that the British navy had declared an illegal blockade of Guadeloupe and Martinique. The American secretary of state contended that this was a mere paper blockade because it could not be effectively enforced. Madison also had pointed out that the blockade had been declared several months before notice of it had reached the United States and that this was burdensome because American vessels bound to the islands could be stopped enroute by the British navy. The chargé admitted the validity of the complaint and reminded the Foreign Office of the controversy that had arisen during the previous war when American vessels had been seized in similar circumstances. Such proceedings, in Thornton's opinion, would promote Anglo-American difficulties that some individuals in the United States would like to exacerbate.[67]

The patience of the long-suffering Thornton was wearing thin as he anxiously awaited the arrival of Merry during the fall of 1803. It was "high time," he wrote the foreign secretary on October 31, for a British minister to arrive in Washington and to restrain those servants of the king such as naval commanders and consuls who were disturbing Anglo-American relations.[68] Thornton's apprehensiveness was justified, for Congress had appointed a committee to investigate the impressment problem and the need to regulate foreign warships in American waters.[69]

Thornton was probably even more disturbed when he learned on Merry's arrival that the new minister had received little forewarning and no instructions on these important matters. Indeed, few ministers ever began a mission with so little guidance. Merry's ministry must be judged with these handicaps in mind. The ability and mettle of any diplomat would have been tested by the handicap of inadequate instructions, the vexing problems of a rapidly escalating maritime war, the difficult living conditions in a raw capital, a controversy over diplomatic etiquette, and the development in the United States of an ill will and a more demanding attitude towards Great Britain that dated,— according to Thornton,—from the time word was first received of the Louisiana Purchase.[70]

III. "A Foolish Circumstance of Etiquette"

Unfortunate personality traits that lessened the effectiveness of both Anthony and Elizabeth Merry as British representatives to the United States were glaringly evidenced in their controversy with American officials over diplomatic etiquette. That dispute arose soon after their arrival, when they concluded that they were not accorded the deference that they considered was due them as English gentlefolk and representatives of His Britannic Majesty.

The affair, for which the Merrys were not solely to blame, has either amused or annoyed historians of Anglo-American relations, in some degree proportionate to their Federalist or Jeffersonian bias. The controversy has hindered an objective appraisal of the situation that Merry encountered at the outset of his American mission and has either given a prejudiced view of his mission or deflected attention from more important matters. Although Henry S. Randall (in his biography of Jefferson) was the first to write in detail concerning the etiquette dispute, Henry Adams's one-chapter treatment of the quarrel is the extensive account that has become best known. While not as friendly in discussing Jefferson's role as Randall, Adams, nevertheless, was generally hostile to the Merrys. The most balanced and comprehensive account is found in Dumas Malone's chapter, "Without Benefit of Protocol: The Merry Affair" in his *Jefferson the President: First Term, 1801–1805.* Yet Malone's account contains a suggestion of bias against Merry when he writes that "the episode clamors for comic treatment and defies rational analysis."[1] In a far less scholarly work than Malone's, Beckles Willson probably describes the affair most accurately as "the tragi-comedy" of the Merrys.[2]

Merry's predilection as an "old diplomat" for being au fait in matters of protocol had led him before leaving England to inquire from his predecessor Robert Liston about practices in the United States.[3] But if Merry wanted to be au fait, Liston was not au

courant, for he had served at Philadelphia under the more ceremonious Federalist regimes of Washington and Adams and was
unacquainted with the democratic, republican style of Thomas
Jefferson. It was the punctilious Merry's misfortune to encounter
a president who not only eschewed elaborate ceremony by preference and design but was also contemptuous of professional
diplomacy. Jefferson, indeed, once wrote, "I have ever considered
diplomacy as the pest of the peace of the world, as the workshop
in which nearly all the wars of Europe are manufactured."[4]

Moreover, it was ill luck for Merry that the absence of feminine
influence in Jefferson's household probably made the widowed
president less attentive to sartorial matters for himself and seat-
ing arrangements for his guests, the two things that first gave
umbrage to Merry. Also Merry had the misfortune to arrive on
the scene when American officials were less inclined to be defer-
ential to Britain and her representatives. The Americans in late
1803 were exulting over the acquisition of Louisiana, and with
Britain and France again at war, they saw no need for courtship
by diplomacy, much less marriage by alliance.

When Merry arrived in America, the new etiquette of informality
had been in effect for nearly two years, but its impact had not
been fully felt by the small diplomatic corps in Washington,
which consisted only of the Spanish minister and the British, Danish,
and French chargés d'affaires. Merry was the first diplomat of
ministerial rank to be received by Jefferson, and he was the first
minister to establish a full-scale legation in Washington, because the
Marqués de Casa Yrujo, the Spanish minister, spent much time in
Philadelphia with the family of his American wife. The corps had
acquiesced in the new etiquette because the chargés benefited
from Jefferson's ignoring distinctions of diplomatic rank. Yrujo had
remained silent, though resentful, concerning the lack of deference
accorded him and had awaited the arrival of Merry as an ally.

Immediately on arrival in Washington, Merry was exposed to the
informality of the new etiquette. The day after he had apprised
the secretary of state of his desire to be presented to the president,
Madison accompanied Merry to the President's House for the
presentation. Being of the old school and not having been warned
by Madison of what to expect sartorially from Jefferson, prim-and-

proper Merry went decked out in full diplomatic dress, which consisted of a coat of deep blue with black velvet trim and gold braid, white breeches, silk stockings, ornate buckled shoes, plumed hat, and a sword. Even the fastidious Foster referred to Merry's costume as having been "bespeckled with the spangles of our gaudiest court dress."[5]

Merry's first shock came when the president was not in the room where Madison expected the presentation to take place. Madison then proceeded to a passageway leading into the president's study. Merry, thinking that the presentation was to take place in another room, followed Madison. At that moment Jefferson entered the opposite end of the passage, and the nonplussed Merry with sword and feathers was forced to back out.[6] In these awkward circumstances, the presentation took place, and Merry delivered the short address that he had laboriously composed and rehearsed. The discomposure of "Toujours Gai," as Augustus J. Foster recounted it a year later, was still greater when he observed that President Jefferson was not dressed in the formal attire that the solemnity of a diplomatic presentation customarily demanded. Merry did not wait for the arrival of Foster to express his resentment but proceeded during the weeks immediately following the presentation to castigate the president's casual dress. The story was undoubtedly savored and somewhat embellished by those Federalists who listened attentively. According to an account written six weeks after the incident by Samuel Taggart, a Federalist congressman from Massachusetts, the president was dressed in gown and slippers when he received Merry. It was rumored, Taggart wrote, that the president even wore his nightcap, but the congressman admitted that rumor was very likely an "hyperbole." Obviously the Federalist reporter was pleased to write that the British minister was not at all charmed with "Democratic Majesty" and was in a dudgeon because of his ill treatment.[7] Merry never forgot nor forgave Jefferson's sartorial offense. Two years after the presentation, he recounted with great asperity the details of that occasion to Josiah Quincy, another Federalist congressman from Massachusetts. Merry recalled that the president's slippers were down at the heels and that his pantaloons, coat, and underclothes generally indicated "utter slovenliness and

THE BRITISH LEGATION AT WASHINGTON, 1803–6

Described by Anthony Merry as "two mere shells" thrown together, these houses on K Street, NW, were the residence of the British minister during his three years in the United States. This photograph shows the two houses as they appeared before demolition in 1961. (Reproduced from Harold Donaldson Eberlain and Cortlandt Van Dyke Hubbard, *Historic Houses of George-Town & Washington City* [1957], p. 343, courtesy of Cortlandt Van Dyke Hubbard.)

indifference to appearances" and were "in a state of negligence, actually studied."[8]

Despite Merry's umbrage over the president's appearance, however, the initial interview with Jefferson was pleasant. Yet the elegantly dressed British minister was astounded when the president of the United States sat down and proceeded to toss a "down at the heel" slipper into the air and catch it on the point of his foot. Apparently this example of presidential informality was still a vivid memory to the astonished Merry when Stratford Canning served as his secretary on a mission to Denmark in 1807 and heard from "Toujours Gai" of his encounter.[9]

While much has been written of the careless dress of Virginia gentlemen and of Jefferson's preference for comfortable clothes, the president was too knowledgeable concerning what was considered fitting dress on such an occasion for his actions not to have been deliberate. But whatever his motive, he and Madison disregarded the feelings of an English gentleman who with his gaudy court dress sought only to show respect for their official position in the conventional way. Courtesy, it seems, would have demanded that Merry at least should have been forewarned.

Soon after Merry's official presentation, Madison informed him that he was expected to make the first visit to all department heads, and not to the secretary of state alone. When Merry protested that this differed from what had been required of Liston, he was told that the rules of diplomatic etiquette previously followed were not precedents that bound the present administration. Despite his protest, Merry acquiesced and made the first visits in order to carry on his official business.[10] Apparently at the same time that Merry protested against making the first visits, he complained about the informality of his official presentation. Madison replied that the Danish chargé had been received in a similar manner, whereupon Merry countered that the Dane was of third rank in the diplomatic hierarchy while he himself belonged to the second. Madison, speaking both for himself and Jefferson, then observed that it was just as preposterous for Merry to insist on social distinctions in the United States as it would be for an American to insist on equality at the Court of St. James's.[11] About the same time that Merry received this jolt, Vice-President Burr advised him that the diplomatic corps would no longer be extended the courtesy of occupying chairs on the floor of the Senate. Burr, however, went out of his way to explain that this was done because of an indiscretion by Yrujo, and consequently Merry did not take offense, though the move came at a bad time for him psychologically.[12] If the president and the secretary of state had also explained their procedure beforehand to Merry, much of the etiquette controversy might have been avoided.

Three days after his presentation to the president, Merry and his wife were invited to the President's House for a dinner that Merry understood was in his honor. Other members of the diplomatic corps present were Yrujo and his American wife, along with Louis André Pichon, the French chargé d'affaires. The presence of Pichon was irregular, for the custom prevailed then as of now of not inviting the diplomatic representatives of countries at war with each other to the same social gathering. But according to Pichon, he was especially invited to be present by Jefferson, who urged the Frenchman to return in time for dinner from Baltimore, where official business had carried him. [13]

To the consternation of the Merrys, not only did they find themselves in the Frenchman's company but the president escorted Mrs. Madison in to dinner and seated her, rather than Mrs. Merry, at the place of honor to his right, even though the former had whispered to Jefferson, "take Mrs. Merry." [14] Foster later wrote that Merry then led his own wife in, but Merry himself wrote that Madison escorted the lady. [15] Other guests were aghast at this departure from custom, though Jefferson had previously recognized no distinctions at his table and had asked cabinet wives to take the place of honor. It is evident that Dolly Madison thought the president had made a faux pas in the case of Mrs. Merry, and years later she recalled that Yrujo's wife in observing the discomfiture of the Merrys on that occasion had exclaimed, "This will be the cause of war." [16] Not only was Mrs. Merry slighted, but Merry himself was ignored when a congressman brushed by and took a place next to the Spanish minister's wife before Merry could sit there. He was even more astonished when the president did not intervene. [17] It would be interesting to know whether this was the same congressman who, when told at Jefferson's table that crawfish were considered a delicacy in Europe, sneeringly remarked to Merry that he thanked God necessity had not driven the Americans to eat such vermin. [18] Wounded and outraged by what he considered were at least boorish manners and at worst deliberate insults, Merry by his own account summoned his carriage as soon as the meal was over and drove off with his irate wife. [19]

In a dispatch of December 6, 1803, to Lord Hawkesbury, Merry described both his initial interview with Jefferson and the dinner at the President's House. While obviously disconcerted and hurt, Merry reported that he intended to take no formal notice of these affronts unless he was instructed to do so. He declared, however, that he would protest if the traditional usage, termed by him "the ancient distinctions," should be followed by the American government in the case of a new minister who might be sent in the future to Washington by some other country. He advised Lord Hawkesbury that the social innovations were deliberate, which indeed they were, and had been put into operation on the occasion of his arrival by the Americans for the purpose of "raising their own consequence" but without any intent of showing disrespect to the British monarch.[20]

But later in the same day, after Merry had written of these incidents and disclaimed any intention of taking official action in the etiquette matter, he and Mrs. Merry were subjected to even greater informality and disregard of their official position at the home of Secretary of State James Madison. Again Mrs. Merry was not honored as the wife of a newly arrived minister could have reasonably expected to be.[21] Madison instead offered his arm to Mrs. Gallatin, and Mrs. Merry was left unattended. With visible indignation, Merry then escorted his wife to the head of the table, whereupon Mrs. Gallatin withdrew in her favor—without, however, being thanked by Mrs. Merry.[22]

What particularly galled the Merrys in this instance was that the Madisons departed from the style they had observed hitherto and followed instead the procedure used by Jefferson—for the widowed president had found it convenient at his house to escort into dinner a cabinet wife who would act as hostess at his table. Pichon's explanation of Madison's departure from the old style was that the secretary of state wished to make Merry feel more keenly the effects of the "uproars" he had caused.[23] The Frenchman's explanation, however, will not suffice, because Merry had not yet publicly revealed his displeasure and, as seen in his dispatch of December 6 to Hawkesbury, had even decided to go along with the style prevailing at the President's House, at least when he was a guest there. Neither Pichon nor Merry perceived that the secretary of state was obliged to conform to the president's style of entertainment whenever the Merrys were involved and thus that Madison did not deliberately seek to offend them.

The dinner at the Madisons was even more unpleasant for all concerned than the president's dinner had been. When Mrs. Merry cattily remarked that the lavish spread looked like a harvest-home supper, the indomitable Dolly replied that it merely reflected the prosperity of America and that abundance was preferable to elegance.[24] The next day, December 7, Merry wrote to his friend George Hammond in the Foreign Office and unbosomed himself. According to Merry, the innovations in etiquette were "evidently from design and not from Ignorance and Awkwardness (though God knows a Great deal of both as to matters even of Common Etiquette is to be seen at every Step)." Merry added that preference was given "in every respect to the wives of the Secretaries (a Set of beings as little without the manners as without the appearance of Gentlewomen). . . . " He concluded that foreign ministers in the United States were placed in a situation so degrading to the countries they represented and so personally disagreeable to themselves as to be almost intolerable.[25]

Merry's reputation in history might have been better if he had stopped with this tirade written to a friend in a private letter, but he did not stop. Brooding over the slights connected with his presentation, the two dinners, and other innovations and difficulties, he talked with Yrujo, members of the Federalist opposition, and anyone else who would listen to his tale of woe regarding the incivility, rudeness, and deliberate insults to which he and Mrs. Merry had been subjected. His complaints reached the ears of the administration, as he undoubtedly hoped they would. Because of Merry's complaints, Madison began to inquire about diplomatic etiquette from knowledgeable people. These inquiries were indeed belated, since they were made after an innovation had been initiated. The secretary of state sought to justify the official position and inquired about British practice from Rufus King, recently returned from England.[26] He probably hoped to gain the support of a prominent Federalist who had well-placed friends in England to whom he might appeal if the British government should take any notice of the etiquette affair.

Madison urged King to reply as soon as possible on whether first visits to the ministers of the crown were made by plenipotentiaries, on what precedence was observed on public occasions and ordinary business, and on whether the same precedence was observed for the ladies as for their husbands. According to Madison,the American officials desired to follow the rule of *pêle-mêle* in social intercourse as far as possible, but he admitted that this might be difficult, since the United States did not wish to be behind other nations. To say the least, Jefferson and Madison had indeed been careless in not raising these questions before their innovations in etiquette were introduced. King's prompt reply, however, indicated that London usage gave little support to Merry's claims and pretensions. Diplomats, said King, were never invited to informal royal parties, and there was no precedence in the queen's drawing room for formal occasions. On other social occasions in England, the ladies entered the dining room with the one of highest title going first.[27]

Although King's report was viewed by the administration as a vindication of its position, it was a fact, nevertheless, that a different procedure had been followed under Washington and Adams, and Merry had not been forewarned of the change, which would have been a prudent course in order to prevent misunderstanding. The Federalists were naturally delighted to sympathize with the disgruntled Merry and to rejoice at the trouble he had made for the administration. When Madison inquired of Timothy Pickering, a former secretary of state, concerning etiquette practice under the former administrations, Pickering acidly replied that General Washington followed a practice opposite to the present administration and that he was remarkable for his correctness.[28]

When Augustus J. Foster became Merry's secretary in late 1804, he concluded that the etiquette affair was of little importance, but he believed that the American officials had deliberately sought to humble the British representatives. Moreover, he was of the opinion that because Jefferson and Madison were both gentlemen, they knew better and hence were awkward in their attempt to humble the British by degrading Merry.[29] The subsequent efforts of Jefferson and Madison to be conciliatory with the Merrys convinced Foster that this was the correct interpretation. The first effort to soothe the wounded feelings of the Merrys came when the Madisons again invited them to dinner, but in a private capacity.

Merry went, but Mrs. Merry stayed at home, though the invitation
had been arranged with her.[30] Learning of Mrs. Merry's botanical
interests, Jefferson sent her a gift of flower seeds, which she politely
acknowledged and even offered to reciprocate, though there is no
record of any exchange.[31] In order to assuage Mrs. Merry's feelings,
the president also discontinued his practice of escorting any of
his lady guests to dinner.[32]

But despite these conciliatory gestures, the Merrys by the end of
December 1803, had decided they would avoid all social occasions
where they might be exposed to any treatment not in accord
with their idea of the deference owed them.[33] Merry accordingly
attended the president's New Year's Day reception for the public,
but Mrs. Merry stayed away. Robert Smith, secretary of the navy,
then invited the Merrys for tea and even contrived to give
Mrs. Merry the place of honor, but she declined the invitation.
The secretary of war, Henry Dearborn, next invited Merry to his
house, but he declined to go. Finally Albert Gallatin, secretary
of the treasury, invited Merry to his home, but he did not appear,
though he had accepted the invitation.[34] Not only did the
Merrys spurn the efforts of the American officials to make amends,
but they took offense anew when they learned of the precedence
given the wife of Jerome Bonaparte, the former Betsy Patterson
of Baltimore, at the President's House. On that occasion in January
1804, when Napoleon's younger brother and his recent bride were
visiting Washington, the president had gallantly offered his hand
to Betsy instead of a cabinet member's wife. The Merrys had
not been able to swallow the president's earlier preference of
Mrs. Madison over Mrs. Merry; much less could they now
accept the wife of a Bonaparte who had scandalized Washington
with her scanty dress, even though she hailed from Baltimore,
and was a niece by marriage of Senator Samuel Smith and
a cousin of Robert Smith, the secretary of the navy.[35]

Although Merry was critical of Yrujo for having acquiesced in
the practice of *pêle-mêle*, and despite his distrust of the don
(whom he had known since his service in Spain and considered "an
insignificant and unsafe character"[36]), he and the Spanish minister
began to act in concert against administrative innovations in
diplomatic etiquette. They agreed between themselves that if they

should ever in the future attend a presidential dinner at the same time (which they never again did) their wives would alternate in occupying the place of honor. They also agreed that at legation dinners to which they might invite cabinet members and their wives, they would escort their own wives to the table. Yrujo, once described by Pichon as "vanity personified," was particularly blamed by the Americans for fanning the flame of Merry's resentment, though the Federalists also played a part.[37]

Amidst all the "buzz"[38]—as Rufus King aptly described what Madison, with poor grace and less taste, correctly called "a foolish circumstance of etiquette"[39]—Jefferson and his cabinet took up the matter and framed the official "Canons of Etiquette," which established the principles of *pêle-mêle* in official society. The canons were officially communicated to Merry about January 12, 1804.[40] In a conference following this, Merry very correctly pointed out that the rules should have been given him on his arrival. When Madison observed that Rufus King had been invited to dinners in London at which his wife was not given preference, Merry rejoined that they were private affairs, whereupon Madison retorted that his dinner on December 6 had also been private.[41] That was hardly the case, for Madison, subsequent to that dinner at which the Merrys had been affronted, specifically invited the Merrys to a private dinner, thereby tacitly admitting that the one on the sixth had not been private.

By the middle of January, Washington society (according to Pichon) had been turned upside down by the etiquette controversy, and the ladies were exasperated by Mrs. Merry as the cause of the commotion.[42] The situation did not improve when she appeared at a ball given by the Robert Smiths in a "brilliant and fantastic" outfit that consisted of

. . . white satin with a long train, dark blue crape of the same length over it and white crape drapery down to her knees and open at one side, so thickly cover'd with silver spangles that it appear'd to be a brilliant silver tissue; a breadth of blue crape, about four yards long, and in other words a long shawl, put over her head, instead of over her shoulders and hanging down to the floor, her hair bound tight to her head and a diamond comb behind, diamond ear-rings and necklace, displayed on a bare bosom.[43]

Obviously if Betsy Patterson Bonaparte went too far in one direction, Mrs. Merry went too far in the other, and the ladies of Washington were equally outraged by both. Mrs. Merry, described as a "large, tall well-made woman" must have made an impressive figure, and the Washington ladies were even more provoked than before. Mrs. Merry did not make matters any easier for herself when the president's daughter, Martha Jefferson Randolph, came to Washington for a visit and Mrs. Merry wrote her a note caustically inquiring whether Mrs. Randolph wished to be treated as the wife of a congressman or as the daughter of the president. Mrs. Randolph, truly her father's daughter, replied that she wished to be treated with no other distinction than that accorded any stranger. [44]

The Federalist press took up the etiquette controversy, and in its reporting either garbled or misrepresented the facts. A greatly exaggerated account of the president's dinner at which the Merrys had been offended appeared in the *Gazette of the United States* of Philadelphia on January 17, 1804, in the form of a letter from Washington dated January 2. That account had it that all the cabinet members and their wives had trooped into dinner and swept by the Merrys, who had been left to look on as the procession went by. According to the writer of the letter, this "unaccountable conduct" could be attributed to "pride, whim, weakness and malignant revenge." That Mrs. Merry had been called upon first by the cabinet wives was explained by Mrs. Madison's not "waiting for orders" from the president. Federalist rancor is evident when the writer recounted the effect of Mrs. Madison's visit on the other wives: "This threw them all into consternation. What was to be done? Could they commit their dignity so much as to wait on Mrs. Merry? After a great deal of parade, and bowing, and whispering, and counselling, some of them came to. Mrs. Secretary Smith paid her visit, a few days later Mrs. Gallatin made her congée, and a few days after that Mrs. Dearborn squatted down in the midst of them." [45]

When the *Washington Federalist* also misrepresented what had taken place by reporting that both cabinet members and their wives outranked diplomats, President Jefferson himself wrote an anonymous reply printed by William Duane on February 13, 1804, in the Philadelphia *Aurora*,[46] a Republican paper. In his reply Jefferson outlined the "Canons of Etiquette" and boldly proclaimed that there had been no "Court of the United States" since March 4, 1801, for "That day buried levees, birthdays, royal parades, processions with white wands, and the arrogance of precedence in society, by certain self-styled friends of order, but truly styled friends of privileged orders."[47] About the same time Jefferson's statement appeared in the *Aurora*, Nathaniel Macon, a rustic congressman from North Carolina and administration leader in the House, wrote that the British minister had "kicked up a little dust" about rank and had spurred Yrujo "to shew a trick or two about this new fangled doctrine of rank, where the people nor their form of government acknowledge any." In a droll vein Macon observed that such pretentious claims of protocol might meet the same fate that claims often met in the House Committee on Claims, viz., "leave to withdraw." Macon thus hinted that the behavior of the two ministers might lead to their involuntary withdrawal from Washington.[48]

But regardless of what Jefferson and Madison may have originally intended, efforts to mollify the Merrys continued. Intermediaries such as Senator George Logan of Pennsylvania and Congressman John Dawson of Virginia were sent to inquire if Merry would dine privately with Jefferson.[49] Merry, however, slammed shut the door to friendlier relations that the president had tried to open. He condescendingly replied that although he already had a social engagement, he would come, provided he was reassured that he was being entertained in a private rather than an official capacity. Merry gave as his excuse for not accepting an official invitation the explanation that he was awaiting a reply from the Foreign Office to his dispatches concerning the various breaches in etiquette. Moreover, Merry compounded his ungracious response to Jefferson by replying, not directly to the president, but to the secretary of state.[50]

Jefferson and Madison were justifiably exasperated by Merry's repulse of their overtures, and Jefferson sarcastically commented to the French chargé that he would be highly honored when the king of England would let Merry come and eat his soup. As a result of Merry's action, he and his wife never again received an invitation to dine with the president. Thus they deprived themselves of not only the company of a brilliant conversationalist but also the food of a gourmet and the wine of a connoisseur. Yet despite Pichon's recognition of Merry's gaucherie, it is significant that he thought the controversy over etiquette could have been avoided if the American officials had prudently forewarned Merry concerning the new style on his arrival.[51] It should not be overlooked that Merry had attempted to acquaint himself beforehand with diplomatic protocol observed in the United States.

Apprehensive that their difficulties with Merry regarding diplomatic etiquette might have undesirable repercussions in America's relations with Great Britain, Jefferson and Madison saw that James Monroe in London received a detailed account of what had happened. In his first dispatch to Monroe touching on the trouble with Merry, Madison on December 26, 1803, emphasized that he considered Merry himself to be amicable and agreeable. Madison blamed the whole affair on Mrs. Merry, but in view of Merry's background Madison's explanation was too simple. With unjustified optimism, Madison also concluded that Merry would eventually overlook the matter, since he would find the American officials sincerely disposed to cultivate cordial relations and to show respect.[52] Jefferson, likewise, declared that Merry was personally acceptable but that his "virago" of a wife was the cause of all the discord. The president even went so far as to declare, albeit before Merry's ungracious response to his second invitation, that the administration would make every effort to reclaim such a "reasonable and good man" for Washington society.[53]

Although it is doubtful that the thin-skinned Merry—even if left alone—would have been so easily reclaimed as Jefferson and Madison intimated, Yrujo and the Federalists saw that he was not left alone. Thus Merry, who at first might have attributed his unfortunate reception to ignorance alone, became more and more certain that it was all a premeditated insult. He accounted for this treatment by pointing out that the Americans were irritated because the British had sent only an envoy to the United States and not an ambassador. It is interesting that Augustus J. Foster, who arrived on the scene later in the year and who thought Merry had probably made too much of the etiquette affair, likewise believed that the Americans wanted an ambassador and one of noble rank.[54] Edward Thornton had earlier recommended that such an appointment would be pleasing to the Americans.[55] And James Madison himself could have been interpreted by Englishmen in 1804 as indicating a desire for an ambassador when, in discussing the Canons of Etiquette with Merry, he had observed that no distinctions would be made among members of the diplomatic corps *unless* there was an ambassador.[56]

When the administration's account of the etiquette affair reached Monroe in February, he said nothing to the British ministers and waited for them to take the initiative. The ministry knew of the matter as early as February 8, for on that date Christopher Gore received word of Merry's difficulties from Lord Hawkesbury. Gore tactfully expressed his regret and advised that the matter be overlooked.[57] The ministry took this tack and to Monroe's surprise said nothing to him.[58] British newspapers published without comment excerpts from Federalist newspapers that pertained to the affair. William Cobbett, however, in the columns of *Cobbett's Weekly Political Register*, reminded Englishmen that he had opposed the appointment of Anthony Merry to the American mission. Merry, he reiterated, was not of equal caliber to the representatives sent to Britain by the United States. Neither was Merry "the sort of person or character Americans like." To Cobbett it was mortifying to risk even the slightest injury to British interest because of a matter so trifling as indignities suffered by the Merrys, about whom nobody had ever heard until they were sent to America.[59]

Although nothing was ever said to Monroe officially, he deduced that the British ministry was nevertheless annoyed by the American reception of Merry. Monroe also thought that because of the etiquette affair he himself had possibly been subjected to some slights. Queen Charlotte ignored him at a court function, but he admitted that the queen was old and because of poor eyesight might not have seen him.[60] By April Monroe had definitely decided to ignore the controversy.[61] Gore, who apparently never discussed the matter with Monroe, also never heard anything further from Hawkesbury.[62] Monroe concluded that the

Foreign Office had instructed Merry to conform,[63] but that is improbable, since there is no evidence whatever in the official
correspondence of a response to Merry's representations on the
subject. It is also possible that the etiquette affair might have
been overlooked, intentionally or otherwise, in the shuffle
attending the fall of the Addington government in May 1804 and
the return of William Pitt to office. Merry—ironically, a strong
Pittite—was thus left out on a limb, which perhaps was best for
all concerned. Monroe generously suggested that Jefferson ignore
the etiquette matter in his message to Congress and somehow
contrive to let Merry know that the American minister in London
had never been instructed to raise the issue with the British government.[64]

Although he never had any official communication with the
British ministry concerning Merry's difficulties, Monroe learned
that some of the ministers had been at the time very much irritated
with the Americans.[65] In July, Lord St. Helens, a well-known
diplomat and a lord in waiting, asked about his old friend
Merry in a manner that did not suggest to Monroe that he had any
knowledge of Merry's troubles in America.[66] But some members of
the professional diplomatic service had more than an inkling of
what had occurred. George Jackson in July 1804 wrote that Merry
in Washington had experienced brutal manners, terrible living
conditions, and pointed hostility to Great Britain.[67] Francis James
Jackson, however, intimated several years later that Merry himself
was to blame for making so much over "a foolish question of
precedence." The latter Jackson, who was Merry's friend and who
was also destined to serve with notable lack of success at Washington, seemed to take pleasure in recounting how in 1809 his wife
was escorted to dinner by President Madison while he himself
escorted Dolly Madison with whom, he said, Mrs. Merry was
"always at daggers drawn."[68]

During the winter of 1803–4 while the unhappy Merry vainly
waited for instructions concerning the etiquette dispute, he and Mrs.
Merry experienced other affronts and inconveniences. The Merrys
were plagued by a desertion of their white servants and were
forced to hire Negro slaves as domestics at the legation. In one
instance Merry hired a slave who belonged to one Henry

Suttle, who was "nothing more than an inferior clerk to a merchant." Suttle sent a constable to recover his slave, and Merry was outraged that the constable violated the diplomatic immunity of His Britannic Majesty's legation and that Suttle had the effrontery to address him as an equal.[69] When Merry complained to the secretary of state, Madison refused to intervene, on the grounds that no contract with Suttle had been signed. Merry was thus left without redress for recovering the servant. Moreover, nothing could be done about the violation of the legation's immunity, because only a Negro slave, whose testimony was inadmissible in the courts, had witnessed the constable's invasion. Merry, however, believed that Suttle went unreprimanded because he was a strong supporter of the Jefferson administration. No wonder Merry fumed that this was still another instance of the unlawful and uncivil proceedings that were too common in America.[70] Neither were his feelings assuaged when he learned that one of his deserting servants had been employed in the household of James Madison.[71]

Madison by the spring of 1804 had concluded that since Merry had not brought up the etiquette business again, he was probably embarrassed by the failure of the British government to support him. Thus Madison continued to hope that the Merrys might yet be drawn from their self-imposed seclusion. The Madisons even invited the Merrys to visit them at Montpellier during the summer, but the invitation was not accepted.[72] Merry, however, did condescend to take his young guest, Thomas Moore the Irish poet, to the President's House for a public reception, but the two were offended when the lanky Jefferson only "stared down" at the diminutive Moore and ignored Merry's guest.[73]

Any headway that might have been made in restoring more amicable relations with the kindly Madison was blasted in the late summer of 1804. While Madison was vacationing at Montpellier in August, Merry complained that a "mere clerk" in the State Department had presumed to correspond with him in Madison's absence from Washington.[74] Merry's petulance in this matter and an irritating exchange of correspondence during August concerning impressment led the secretary of state to conclude that the British minister was a "mere Diplomatic pettifogger."[75] Yet some degree of social contact continued between Madison and Merry, for in the summer of 1805, while Mrs. Madison and the Merrys were in Philadelphia undergoing medical treatment, Madison and Merry exchanged greetings.[76]

But Merry never ceased brooding over the earlier slights. When Foster arrived to be his secretary at the end of 1804, Merry rehashed the whole story of the etiquette controversy.[77] His pique was again aroused at the president's New Year reception in 1806, when Jefferson only bowed to Merry and bestowed more attention on a delegation of visiting Indian chieftains. Declaring that he would not be treated thus and taking care that Senator George Logan overheard his remark, Merry departed in high dudgeon.[78] A few weeks later Merry again took umbrage when on February 15 John Quincy Adams introduced a bill in the Senate to prevent the abuse of the privileges and immunities enjoyed by foreign ministers within the United States. Adams's proposal, occasioned by the offensive conduct of Yrujo, the Spanish minister, empowered the president to order the withdrawal of any minister who might show disrespect, commit any hostility, or conspire against the United States. Merry wailed to the Foreign Office that this proposal was still another example of what he had earlier complained about to Lord Hawkesbury, viz., the American government's determination to abolish all respect and distinctions owed diplomats assigned to the United States. Although the proposed bill was rejected by the Senate five days after he complained to the foreign secretary, Merry never apprised his government of that fact.[79]

Even after receiving notice of his recall, Merry and his wife experienced fresh grievances from what they considered American boorishness. In July 1806, Augustus J. Foster wrote that Mrs. Merry had recently relented and attended a social function at the Madisons, where—to her horror—she encountered none other than her haberdasher as a fellow guest. One can imagine what her reaction might have been if she could have foreseen that later in the nineteenth century a onetime tailor would occupy the President's House, as would an ex-haberdasher in the twentieth. Yet on remembering her background and pride, one can nevertheless sympathize with Elizabeth Merry when reading Foster's account. He related how she continued to be criticized for her gowns, which were sometimes trod upon, and how she would return to the legation in tears.

On one occasion, when the Merrys were invited to a ball at an inn in Georgetown given by the "Democrats" to celebrate the acquisition of Louisiana, Mrs. Merry, who had "put on her best as a compliment" to a national affair, was met at the door and told that her "undemocratic diamonds" must be removed. Not only was Mrs. Merry subjected to indignities away from the British legation, but even at her own assemblies boorish guests wore muddy boots and disheveled dress. Foster's exclamation, "Think of a fine woman accustomed to adulation, coming here as a wife to the minister of one of the first countries in the world," and his rhetorical question, "Were you so placed, how would your feelings have been shattered?" do arouse sympathy, though an American might bristle at his conclusion, "It is indeed a country not fit for a dog."[80]

But while one may sympathize and agree that the Merrys on occasion were sinned against, they brought much of their trouble on themselves. Their touchy dispositions, patronizing ways, and hauteur raised American hackles but did not justify the boorishness to which they were sometimes unquestionably subjected. Undoubtedly Merry's mission to the United States was made more difficult because of the controversy over etiquette. Yet the controversy did not hasten the coming of the War of 1812, as some writers have rather extravagantly claimed.[81] Henry Adams went too far when he wrote that the etiquette controversy "left distinct marks of acrimony in the diplomacy of America and England, until war wiped out the memory of reciprocal annoyances.[82]

IV.   Defender of a Vital British Interest

As Anthony Merry surveyed the Anglo-American relationship in 1803, he must have recognized that the greatest concern of his tenure as British minister to the United States would inevitably be maritime affairs. Merry's upbringing and his long experience in the consular service naturally prompted him to give close attention to British naval, shipping, and trading interests, the foundations of British prosperity and power. But the maritime needs of Britain in wartime demanded that a British minister defend his country's interest with special efficiency and vigilance.

Of these maritime needs, the manning of the hard-pressed British navy after 1793, when Britain entered the wars of the French Revolution, had made for serious difficulties in Anglo-American relations because of the frequent impressment of American seamen. Although Merry had not received any instructions concerning the impressment issue, he did have some inkling of the problem from his conference with James Monroe before leaving England. Moreover, he had the benefit of information acquired from Edward Thornton, who, because of his consular service in the United States since 1793, was well acquainted with the difficult problem.

The impressment problem in Anglo-American relations grew in both magnitude and intensity during the French Revolutionary and Napoleonic wars. During the first war some 2410 American seamen were said to have been impressed into the British naval service between 1793 and 1802, and during the second conflict an additional 6057 were allegedly impressed from 1803 until the beginning of the War of 1812.[1] The significant increase of impressments during the latter period and the ensuing bitterness in Anglo-American relations stemmed mainly from the greater manpower requirements of the British navy. Yet economic and political considerations also have to be taken into account in understanding the controversy.

Many Americans believed that British impressments were also

designed to injure the rapidly growing American merchant marine. On the British side, some observers thought that the issue was deliberately magnified by the American administration for domestic political reasons, and some even suspected that the Americans sought an altercation with Britain as a way of ingratiating the United States with Napoleon, who might influence Spain to yield up the Floridas. Moreover, some Englishmen, including Anthony Merry, believed that the United States seized on the impressment issue as a way of forcing the British, so hard pressed navally, to make concessions to American shipping and trade. All of these contentions had some degree of validity, but no American administration, Federalist or Jeffersonian, could fail to have a tender regard for the rights of American seamen based on upholding the honor of national sovereignty as well as humanity and justice.

Anthony Merry had to deal with the impressment problem almost immediately after his arrival. What, might it be asked, was his role in the disputes between Britain and the United States over impressment? How did he influence British policy, and how did he contribute to the amelioration or exacerbation of the impressment problem? In his first dispatch to the Foreign Office, ten days after reaching the American capital, Merry reported that in three different interviews Secretary of State Madison had alluded to the incidence of British impressments not only on the high seas but even in the ports and territorial waters of the United States.[2]

Merry's evaluation of the matter in his first dispatch showed little insight as to why impressment was such a sensitive issue with the Americans. He overlooked the humanitarian and libertarian element completely and implied that the Americans were seizing an opportunity to promote their own commerce and shipping by protesting the impressment of British seamen from their merchant marine. Madison emphasized the American view that the United States flag protected all seamen aboard a ship from removal, with the exception of men in the military service of an enemy. Merry noted, however, that while Madison was emphatic in setting forth the American view, he was temperate and conciliatory.[3] Madison likewise was pleased with the attitude of Merry, who listened attentively to the secretary of state and who, despite his strong defense of the British interest, indicated a willingness to work for some kind of arrangement acceptable to both countries. Concluding, apparently, from Merry's attitude that such an arrangement would have a good chance of acceptance, Madison forwarded the draft of a proposal to Monroe in London.[4]

While Madison and Merry were discussing the impressment problem, Congress was also discussing the matter. Committees had been appointed in November to consider the matter, and in response to a request for information, President Jefferson on December 5 sent to Congress a list of seamen who had been impressed from American merchant vessels. In January 1804, bills for the protection of American seamen were introduced both in the Senate and the House. The Senate bill denied hospitality to any foreign warship that had taken American seamen on the high seas. To Merry such a measure would have an "absolutely hostile Tendency." He informed Madison that if the proposed legislation passed, any negotiation with Britain concerning impressment would cease.

Madison, however, played the matter down by telling Merry that while the president had to respond to the request of Congress for information, the report had been presented in as uninflammatory a manner as possible. The secretary also said that he did not think the legislation would pass, though Merry predicted, erroneously as it turned out, that it would. Merry believed that the bills had been initiated, not in response to popular clamor, but "solely by the unfriendly Disposition of the executive whose influence was so great with Congress."[5] Merry could not believe that Madison knew as little about the bills as he pretended, especially when he defended the bills by saying that British impressments and other offenses had occurred within American jurisdiction.[6] Because Senator Samuel Smith of Maryland, an administration supporter, sponsored the legislation, Merry's suspicions were aroused even more. Yet Merry was wrong in his assumptions, for both Madison and Jefferson thought that the legislation was poorly timed. Congress seemingly agreed, because in late February the matter was postponed until the December session, in order to give the negotiations with Britain a chance.[7]

That Merry deliberately misrepresented the impressment situation solely because of his pique over the etiquette controversy in which he was concurrently involved with the administration is unlikely. Given the circumstances, his suspicions of the administration were justified, for there was widespread anti-British feeling in both official and unofficial circles. Thornton, who had generally enjoyed good relations with the Americans, concurred with Merry that the administration was culpable. Thornton even went so far as to say that he was "scarcely able to credit his senses" in observing the great change that had occurred in Anglo-American relations since the purchase of Louisiana. It appeared to Thornton that the administration was promoting the impressment issue in order to win political favor with the seafaring population of the northern states. Because of this domestic political angle, Thornton counseled firmness but cautioned his superiors against resorting to undue harshness in dealing with the Americans.[8]

But despite the acrimonious discussion of the impressment issue during the winter of 1803-4, there was no immediate prospect of retaliatory legislation in the United States. Recognizing that the desertion of British seamen to the American merchant marine was an underlying reason for many of the impressments, Merry was increasingly concerned about the frequency of such desertions. Perhaps this struck him more forcibly when he recalled that the frigate *Phaeton*, which brought him to Norfolk, lost fourteen men by desertion in that port.[9] In April 1804, he reported to Lord Hawkesbury that twelve British vessels had been recently delayed at Norfolk because of the loss of seamen. According to Col. John Hamilton, the British consul at that port, many of the deserters had joined the United States squadron fitting out for service in the Mediterranean. Merry advised the Foreign Office that on the basis of Hamilton's report he had made a verbal protest to Madison regarding the matter, as a countercharge to Madison's complaints concerning impressment, and had requested the consul to send a description of the deserters to the Admiralty. A few weeks later Merry complained to Madison that six British seamen who had deserted their ship at Charleston had also entered the United States navy. When Madison responded that he could do nothing, because the men had entered voluntarily, Merry concluded that this was in retaliation for the Admiralty's practice of not returning men who had voluntarily taken the king's bounty.[10] Merry not only complained about deserters entering the American service, but he also expressed concern regarding the extent to which American laws either permitted desertion or were not enforced when British captains sought to recover their men. In the Charleston incident a warrant had been issued for apprehending the men, but a United States naval officer prevented its execution, and Madison refused to take any action unless he was assured of a reciprocal restoration of American deserters who had entered the British service, of whom there were very few.[11]

If the recovery of British deserters was made difficult and if the practice of impressing men from neutral vessels on the high seas and in foreign ports was challenged by the United States, there was certain to be opposition to impressment from British merchant vessels in American ports and territorial waters. Although British men-of-war had occasionally impressed seamen within American territorial waters before Merry's arrival, the first instance after he reached Washington occurred in June 1804, when a British naval force arrived off New York. That force was watching two French frigates that had arrived at New York on May 24 from Guadeloupe. The British frigate *Cambrian* and the sloop *Driver* arrived on June 16 and were soon joined by the frigate *Boston*.[12] During the six months that the British watch was maintained—from June to November—Anthony Merry had to deal with the impressment problem and with other matters as well. These included disputes pertaining to the conduct of the British vessels, such as the violation of American revenue and quarantine regulations, the observance of the rule requiring a belligerent vessel in a neutral port to allow twenty-four hours to elapse before pursuing the departing vessel of another belligerent, and the use of American waters as an operating station. In these matters Merry was drawn into discussions with American officials, British naval officers, and Thomas Barclay, the British consul at New York, that had important consequences.

The *Cambrian* and *Driver* reached New York about the same time that the two French frigates were ready to sail. The situation was made even more tense by the fact that Jerome Bonaparte was on one of the frigates. On behalf of the French captains, the mayor of New York—DeWitt Clinton—requested the British vessels on June 17 to allow the customary twenty-four hours to elapse before they sailed in pursuit.[13] The British officers declined on the grounds that they were under orders to sail immediately after delivering dispatches and had already stated their intention to sail before receiving the French request. Barclay, however, referred the matter to Merry in Washington.[14] As a consequence of the British refusal to recognize the twenty-four hour rule in this instance, all pilots in New York harbor were forbidden by Clinton to pilot the British warships until that period of time had elapsed following the departure of the French.[15]

On the same day that Clinton made his request to the British consul concerning the twenty-four hour rule,[16] another, more serious problem arose when a British merchant vessel, the *Pitt* from Greenock, was boarded in New York harbor by a party from the *Cambrian*, which impressed fourteen British seamen. In addition to that violation of American sovereignty, the British violated the harbor quarantine laws by boarding the *Pitt* before she had been cleared by the health officer and by refusing to allow the revenue officer to come aboard. While Consul Barclay upheld the contention of Capt. William Bradley of the *Cambrian* as to the inapplicability of the twenty-four hour rule, he expressed strong disapproval of impressing seamen in New York harbor and violating its quarantine and revenue regulations.[17]

Within a week an account of these violations had reached the secretary of state, who summoned Merry for a conference. When Madison demanded an immediate return of the men impressed, an apology, and delivery of the responsible naval officer for trial in an American court, Merry countered that he had no direct authority over the naval officer involved and that Madison had received an account of only one side of the incident. Since he had received no instructions on the subject of impressment, Merry was of the opinion that the matter should be referred directly to the British government in London by the American minister. In the same conference with Madison in which the *Pitt* affair was discussed, however, Merry protested against the New York attempt to enforce the twenty-four hour rule by denying pilot service to the British naval vessels. This action Merry construed as being an act of partiality. Madison rejected this interpretation by contending that since the British naval officers had already resorted to violence in the harbor, they might have compounded that violence by attacking the French if they had been served by the pilots.[18]

Despite the unsatisfactory outcome of the conference between Madison and Merry, the British minister did advise the British captains at New York to stay as far from American jurisdiction as was possible in keeping with the needs of the naval service. Merry, however, said nothing about the men who had been impressed. His silence disappointed Barclay, who had hoped that Merry would take a stronger stand, more in keeping with his own. Barclay held that regardless of the need for seamen, British warships had no right to impress even British subjects from a British ship when it was in American jurisdiction.[19]

Shortly after his first conversation with Merry on the New York affair, Madison began to complain about other aspects of British naval operations off New York. On July 3 Madison claimed that the British warships were using American waters as an operating station. He also complained that because the *Cambrian* was still off New York, it was evident that the frigate was not on the eve of departure, as had been claimed when the application of the twenty-four hour rule was attempted. Moreover, Madison suggested that if the British continued their operations off New York, the United States would have to take precautions, but he did not say what they might be.[20] Continued impressments by the force off New York—though not within American territorial waters—drew further complaints from Madison. The secretary went on to say that the situation at New York was almost as if that port were under blockade.[21]

In his dispatches on the developments at New York, Merry warned the Foreign Office of the "temper and ill disposition" of Madison, who used "high language accompanied by some degree of menace." Merry speculated that the "menace" or "precautions" threatened by Madison might consist of excluding British warships from American waters. In accounting for both American hostility towards the British and their partiality toward the French, Merry surmised that the United States might be seeking French help in the acquisition of West Florida from Spain. He also thought that the United States might be seeking to force the British

into making some concessions to American commerce and navigation.[22]

In contrast with Merry, Thomas Barclay was increasingly alarmed
by the incidence of British impressments in American waters, some
of which were definitely occurring within the territorial limits of
the United States. On August 14 Barclay wrote Merry that he
had succeeded in suppressing the publication of two affidavits by
American shipmasters that their vessels had been boarded within the
three-mile limit by the frigate *Leander*, which had replaced
the frigate *Boston* in the watch off New York.[23] By this time Merry
had left Washington to obtain medical treatment at Philadelphia,
where he arrived in an exhausted physical and mental state.
But despite his exhaustion, Merry was able to decide on August 15
that the British commanders at New York were justified in
impressing British seamen from a British merchant vessel even
when it was within American territorial waters. He contended that
this had been the practice of foreign warships when he served
as British consul at Malaga. At the same time that Merry informed
Madison of this conclusion, he charged that a French frigate at
Baltimore had impressed seamen in that port several months before
without any objection from the United States.[24] It was when Madison
received the note of August 15 containing these observations that
he indignantly called Merry a "mere Diplomatic pettifogger."[25]

Although both Edward Thornton and Phineas Bond, the British
consul at Philadelphia, agreed with Merry that seamen could be
impressed from a British vessel in a foreign port, Thomas Barclay
strongly opposed that conclusion.[26] In fact Barclay had already
expressed his opposition in a letter to the Foreign Office as early
as June 27. Barclay had also written to Admiral Mitchell, the
commanding officer of the British North American Squadron,
that regardless of what might have been done in some foreign
ports, such impressments were contrary to the "old established
law of nations." Barclay, it might be observed, though a Loyalist
during the Revolution, was a native of America and perhaps
understood American sensitivity in a way that Merry and Thornton
did not. By August 10, the Foreign Office not only had heard
from Barclay but had agreed with his interpretation and had
caused the Admiralty to disapprove Captain Bradley's conduct.[27]

This disapproval came none too soon, for on August 24 Barclay reported to Merry that he knew of four cases in which American ships had been boarded by British press gangs within American territorial limits.[28]

Although Merry had defended Captain Bradley's action in impressing seamen from British ships in American waters, he urged him on August 25 to refrain from impressing men from American or foreign vessels in American jurisdiction.[29] Madison, however, was exasperated by Merry's defense of Bradley. He wrote the British minister on September 3 that because of his upholding the actions of the British naval commanders, there was no advantage in continuing the discussions, which would be transferred to London—a course that Merry had recommended at the beginning of the controversy.[30] With no instruction to guide him, Merry, on the basis of what he recollected was naval practice years before in a Spanish port, courageously defended the British national interest. This was done in the face of what he called the "unjust and violent manner" of the party newspapers supporting the administration. According to Merry, these organs had inflamed the minds of certain elements in the United States against Great Britain by their mischievous language and gross misrepresentation of fact.[31]

While, at the request of the Foreign Office, the Admiralty on August 10 had disapproved Captain Bradley's conduct and had recalled him, Lord Harrowby, the foreign secretary, did not send Merry any instructions on impressment until November 7.[32] In his instructions to Merry of that date, Harrowby upheld Merry's rejection of Madison's claim that the United States flag on the high seas should protect all individuals sailing on American merchant vessels, a "Pretension . . . too extravagant to require any serious refutation." Harrowby, however, did not uphold Merry's view that British men-of-war could impress seamen from British merchant vessels in American ports. Merry was informed that without delay "strictest orders" would be given British naval commanders to observe the utmost lenity in visiting ships on the high seas and to abstain from impressing in the ports of the United States. Acknowledging on February 14, 1805, the receipt of this, his first instruction concerning impressment, Merry promised "strict obedience."[33]

Merry's last involvement with the *Pitt* incident at New York came in June 1805, when he sought to mollify Madison after the secretary of state had learned that Captain Bradley, formerly of the *Cambrian*, had been appointed to the command of a ship of the line. To Madison it seemed that such a promotion might cause other officers to think that the violation of neutral rights was condoned. Merry could only remind Madison that he had never acquiesced in the validity of all the charges brought against Captain Bradley. He also pointed out that the recall of Captain Bradley for inquiry was in itself a mark of disapprobation and that commanding a ship of the line might even be considered a disadvantage, since the chance for prize money was less in that case than for commanding a frigate, which was more often engaged in cruising.[34]

Merry's principal involvement with the impressment issue was during the first year of his American mission, though there were some American complaints in 1805 and 1806. After September 1804, when Madison accused Merry of being a defender of the British naval officers at New York, the State Department had bypassed Merry and presented its complaints to the British government through the American minister in London. But Madison apparently decided that was too circuitous a procedure, and in March 1805, he resumed the discussion of impressment cases with Merry.[35] And, curiously, it was not until April 1805 that Madison (as Merry reported to the foreign secretary) finally asserted in writing what he had always maintained orally: that the United States did not recognize the legality of Britain's claim that the king's subjects could be impressed lawfully from American ships on the high seas.[36] Madison's assertion came as a result of the increased tension after the British sloop of war *Busy* impressed seamen from American vessels outside New York harbor, though not within American territorial limits.[37]

With the resumption of discussions between Madison and Merry concerning impressments, British officials charged that attempts were being made in the United States to protect deserting British seamen by furnishing them with certificates falsely declaring that the seamen were native Americans. In April 1805, Madison protested that the charge made at New York by Consul Barclay that there were about as many British subjects furnished with certificates from American sources as there were Americans was "a very unexpected and unwarranted assertion." Madison complained that this was an "assertion . . . manifestly incredible and disrespectful." Merry candidly admitted that Barclay's remarks were not justified, but he appealed to Madison's candor to acknowledge the fact that illegal certificates of protection were frequently issued.[38] He did, however, take up with Barclay the matter of his sweeping charge, but the consul remained unabashed and unrepentant.[39]

After these exchanges of April 1805 with Madison, Merry never again received any American complaints pertaining to specific instances of impressment. In May 1806, discussion of the subject shifted to London when James Monroe and William Pinkney began their negotiations. Merry's receiving no particular complaints from the spring of 1805 to the spring of 1806 may have been the result of the Admiralty's order of late 1804 to observe lenity, but it could also have reflected Merry's restraining influence on British naval commanders in American waters. Perhaps also the American government decided for its own reasons to temper its representations on impressment in 1805, when Jefferson became aware that the policy of ingratiating the United States with France to the detriment of Anglo-American relations had not succeeded. In late 1805 Merry detected a new tone in his relations with American officials, who now hinted at some sort of Anglo-American cooperation against France and Spain.

But by January 1806, this diplomatic flirtation was over and Congress was discussing other maritime grievances, especially the seizure of American shipping, as well as the problem of impressment. Jefferson, in a special message to Congress on January 17, stated that American "remonstrances" against impressment had "never been intermitted." Despite the absence of complaints to Merry after the spring of 1805 concerning impressments, the president declared in his message that though impressments had diminished in distant seas, they still occurred frequently in American waters.[40] As a result of the general clamor against Britain, the secretary of state was directed to make another report on the number of American citizens impressed since his report of the year before. A bill was proposed in the Senate declaring any person a pirate and felon who impressed a seaman from an American vessel. The bill also provided that it would be lawful to shoot or kill such a person seeking to impress a seaman and that any seaman resisting impressment would be given a reward of $200. Furthermore, in the event that an American citizen was killed or suffered corporal punishment while being impressed, the president was required to levy "the most rigorous and exact retaliation" on the subjects of the responsible government. Any impressed American seaman was to be paid an indemnity of $60 per month from attachments levied on property owned in America by nationals of the government sanctioning impressment. Although Merry thought the bill was ridiculous and impractical and was unlikely to pass, he believed that Congress would approve a modified anti-impressment measure.[41] That, however, did not happen; the Monroe-Pinkney negotiations were authorized instead, and the Non-Importation Act was passed in April 1806.

During Merry's remaining months in America, the only matter relating to impressment that concerned him was that the abuse continued of the issuing of false certificates of protection to British-born seamen employed in the American merchant marine. Soon after Admiral Berkeley's arrival on the Halifax station in June 1806, he forwarded to Merry five examples of such certificates. Merry sent them to Madison with the following comment on the seriousness of the problem:

. . . these documents, being all of a recent date, afford a strong proof of the facility and small expence with which Protections to Foreigners are still granted by the Collectors of Customs in United States ports, notwithstanding that the abuse in this practice has given occasion for such frequent complaints on the part of H. M. Government, and has rendered more necessary the rigorous exercise of His Majesty's just right of reclaiming His subjects from Foreign Service, the exercise of which right has from the Distress and hardships which it is alleged to have brought on the American trade, produced remonstrances from the United States and those discussions now pending in England. . . .[42]

Later in the month, when reporting to Charles James Fox, the foreign secretary, on Berkeley's representation—which he had passed on to Madison—Merry dilated on the alleged number of Englishmen serving in the American merchant marine, many of whom were covered by fraudulent protections. He also alluded to a report he had received that two-thirds of the noncommissioned officers and seamen in the Mediterranean squadron of the United States were foreigners, most of whom were British. Merry commented that this fact had even been confessed to him by some of the American naval officers.[43] In almost his last dispatch from America, Merry was still presenting evidence on the number of British seamen serving in American vessels and cited a report that of the 140 men on the *Syren*, an American sloop of war, all but fourteen were British-born subjects.[44] Undoubtedly reports such as these stiffened the resistance of those in authority in England against making concessions on the impressment issue.

Although the desertion problem and the matter of fraudulent protections and their relation to impressment remained a concern to Merry, the impressment problem, as noted before, was somewhat in the background in his dealings with the American government after 1804. Of greater concern to Merry during the winter and spring of 1804-5 was not impressment by His Majesty's ships but their reception in American ports. As a result of British naval conduct at New York during the summer of 1804, Congress in December of that year took up again the matter of foreign men-of-war within American jurisdiction.[45] On March 3, 1805, an act was passed providing for the possible arrest, with the aid of military force if necessary, of persons who had taken refuge on foreign armed ships in American ports when they were guilty of such offenses as impressing American citizens. Moreover, the president was empowered to bar foreign vessels from American ports if he deemed that their conduct warranted such action. The use of force was also authorized to compel observance of this provision. The act also provided that officers of a foreign armed vessel committing trespass aboard American vessels on the high seas were subject to legal action if apprehended in the United States.[46]

Merry was disturbed by the implications of this act, especially the degree to which customs collectors in American ports might have discretion in the matter and whether impressing seamen from American merchantmen might be considered a trespass. Madison gave Merry no real satisfaction on these points and observed that the collectors would be governed by directives from the president. According to Madison, Congress had given the president in that act discretionary power that he would not use unless there was provocation.[47]

Directions were not given to the collectors and marshals until late May, and Merry concluded in the meantime that the administration really did not intend to execute all provisions of the law unless circumstances should demand execution. Recognizing that such circumstances were contingent on the actions of the British naval commanders, Merry urged the admiral commanding the North American Squadron to order his officers "to act with the utmost Temper, moderation and Forbearance."[48] When on June 11 Madison finally sent Merry copies of the regulations issued to the collectors and marshals, he emphasized again that it was his government's intention to enforce the coercive and penal provisions of the law only when circumstances compelled their enforcement.[49] The forbearance of the American government in the enforcement of the law of 1805 and the easing off of the impressment issue tended to confirm Merry's surmise that the Americans exaggerated their grievances against the British navy, especially in the matter of impressments. This exaggeration, Merry suspected, was intended not only to please the French by beating the drums against the British but also to prod the latter into making commercial concessions as a way of placating the Americans.

If there was little complaint about impressment during 1805 and early 1806, there was none concerning other actions of British men-of-war off the American coast and in American territorial waters. Merry later testified that during that period British warships visited American ports only on three or four occasions. Yet in his annual message to Congress in December 1805, Jefferson mentioned that American commerce was being annoyed by the public and private armed ships of the belligerents hovering off the coasts and harbors of the United States.[50]

In 1805, however, French privateers were probably a more active annoyance to shipping in American coastal waters than were British men-of-war. Indeed, Merry had complained to Madison earlier in the year, when a British ship had been captured off Charleston and brought into that port by a French privateer who sold the vessel without a legal condemnation. In that instance, Madison expressed disapproval of the act.[51]

In January 1806, a few weeks after Jefferson's message in which the marauders were mentioned, Merry again complained that another British ship, the *Esher*, had been captured off the Charleston bar in late 1805 and had been carried to the St. Marys River, between Georgia and Spanish Florida. The vessel was then condemned in most irregular proceedings in Florida and was sold illegally across the river in the town of St. Marys, Georgia.[52] Madison at once responded to Merry's complaint and ordered the collector at St. Marys to investigate.[53] Merry, however, failed to get any satisfaction in the matter, for the collector had allowed the ship to sail as an American vessel from St. Marys, on the grounds that it had been bought by an American.[54] Completely frustrated in the matter, Merry could only report the incident to Fox and say that he expected to receive no further word from the American government on the subject.[55]

On the same day that Merry reported the case of the *Esher* to Fox, he was summoned to a conference with Madison regarding the most serious incident involving a British man-of-war in American waters prior to the *Chesapeake-Leopard* affair of 1807. The incident occurred on April 25, 1806, when the British frigate *Leander*, in firing a warning shot at an American coasting vessel within American territorial waters, accidentally killed the helmsman of the coaster. The *Leander* had arrived at Sandy Hook the day before and had been joined by the frigate *Cambrian* and the sloop *Driver*—those two vessels, like the *Leander*, having been at New York in 1804 when the seamen were impressed from the British ship *Pitt* in New York harbor. The appearance of the three vessels off New York in April 1806 was apparently by accident rather than by plan. The *Leander* came from Bermuda to pick up dispatches, the *Driver* came from Halifax, and the *Cambrian* was cruising in the vicinity. But whatever the reason that brought them together at New York, they proceeded to stop, search, and seize American vessels, often within American territorial waters. The *Leander,* commanded by Capt. Henry Whitby, was particularly culpable, since the shot that had killed the American was fired from the frigate.

The situation at New York in late April was complicated by the fact that when the incident occurred, officers from the *Cambrian* and the *Leander* were ashore picking up dispatches and procuring provisions. The officers were prevented from returning to their vessels by a mob protesting the death of the American seaman. Complicating the situation still further was the fact that an election was in progress in New York, and each side vied with the other in protesting the British outrage. The atmosphere became even more tense when it was learned that three American vessels coming into the harbor had been detained by the frigates and sent to Halifax for adjudication.[56]

When Merry met with Madison on May 3, he leaned that President Jefferson had already determined to issue a proclamation under authority of the law of March 3, 1805. The proclamation closed American ports to the *Cambrian, Driver,* and *Leander* and declared that their officers would be subject to arrest if found within the jurisdiction of the United States. Madison coupled the killing of the seaman with the charge that the three British vessels had in effect been blockading the port of New York.

Merry, who had just received an account of the affair from Consul Barclay in New York when summoned by Madison, contended that there was no blockade of New York. He observed that the three vessels had met there by accident, that the *Driver* had already gone, and that the *Cambrian* and *Leander* would have departed if their officers had not been detained ashore. Merry then proceeded to express regret for what had happened and promised an investigation. He also alluded to the volatile election atmosphere in New York City and intimated that the president's proclamation was unduly severe, if not premature.

Madison did not dispute the justice of Merry's observation about the election. He also admitted that he knew nothing about the detention of the officers and said there was no objection to their returning to their ships. Madison did contend, however, that under the law the president had to issue a proclamation, but that he had not applied all of the provisions. Moreover, Madison stated that he supposed the captain of the *Leander* would take care not to risk apprehension under civil law by going ashore. Merry was quick to note that in his discussion of the *Leander* incident the secretary of state was restrained both in manner and language. Madison did conclude a few days later, however, that Captain Whitby of the *Leander* was guilty of homicide and should either be delivered up to American officials or be punished by British authority. In reply, Merry stated that he would refer the matter to the commanding officer at Halifax and to authorities in London.[57]

In the *Leander* incident Jefferson and Madison were evidently pleased with Merry's reaction. Jefferson wrote Congressman Jacob Crowninshield on May 13 that the United States government had received from the British minister "the most solemn assurances" that the appearance of the three British warships off New York at the same time was entirely accidental and that they would not remain there. Jefferson readily admitted that the situation at New York had been "overdone with electioneering views," although the affair had been "an atrocious violation of . . . territorial rights." The president even admitted that the question of what to do with British warships was a difficult one. Sending the three men-of-war away, he said, was one suggestion that he had followed. Jefferson also pointed out that in the *Leander* incident the American government would emphasize its forbearance in order to obtain better terms for the future.[58] Undoubtedly the president had in mind the Monroe-Pinkney negotiations soon to begin in London. In no wise did Merry's conduct in the *Leander* incident inflame the situation to the detriment of those negotiations, since his conciliatory but firm defense of the British interest did not antagonize Jefferson and Madison.

On the same day as his initial conference with Madison concerning the *Leander* and before he reported the incident to Fox, Merry wrote to Consul Barclay at New York. In his report to the foreign secretary, Merry wrote that he had requested Barclay to communicate at once with the captains of the *Leander*, *Cambrian*, and *Driver,* as well as with the commanding officer of the North American Squadron and to urge these officers "to act with the utmost moderation and circumspection" while they were in the vicinity of New York and to abstain from cruising within the territorial waters of the United States. In his discussions with Madison, Merry had only expressed regret for what had occurred, since he had received no accounts from Whitby and the other captains disproving the American contention that the incident had taken place in American waters.[59]

Before receiving Merry's dispatch concerning the *Leander* affair, Fox in London had learned of the incident. He instructed Merry to express regret to the American government and to say that an investigation would be made, thus confirming the course that Merry had already taken in his discussions with Madison.[60] Insofar as Merry was concerned, the matter ended when he received Fox's instruction of June 6, which he read to Madison. Although Merry and Madison had succeeded in keeping the exchange concerning the *Leander* within bounds of restraint and propriety, Merry privately considered that the government of the United States had acted in a "harsh and severe manner," thus indicating a singular lack of understanding on his part.[61]

The last incident with which Merry was concerned involving an infraction of American territorial sovereignty by a British man-of-war did not have the consequences that he expected. On September 14, 1806, the British frigates *Belleisle, Bellona,* and *Melampus*—while chasing the French ship *L'Impetueux*—caused that vessel to run aground near Norfolk. The British captors then proceeded to burn the vessel and bring the crew as prisoners to Norfolk. Merry must have been extremely apprehensive of what might follow in the United States from the occurrence of this incident so soon after the *Leander* incident. When he apprised the Foreign Office of the occurrence near Norfolk, he warned that a great hue and cry would be raised against that violation of American territorial sovereignty. But to Merry's surprise, no notice was taken of the incident by Madison, who apparently received no protest from the French government until after Merry had returned to England.[62]

The violation of American territorial sovereignty by the British navy and the impressment of American seamen were not the only maritime matters with which Anthony Merry was involved during his mission to the United States. It will be recalled that one of the Anglo-American problems about which Merry had received no instructions and that had greatly disturbed Christopher Gore was the matter of American trade to blockaded enemy ports. Gore was especially worried about the ports of St. Domingue, where the French in 1803 were attempting to restore their control. Involved in the matter was the question of the legitimacy of a blockade if a naval force was not actually present. Likewise involved were the circumstances—particularly the timing—under which a blockade was declared. Closely related also was the old problem of whether enemy ports, especially those of colonies, could be opened to neutral trade during a war when they had been closed in time of peace.

The issue soon arose—just as Gore had feared it would. On December 24, 1803, about a month after Merry's arrival in Washington, Madison complained about a general blockade of St. Domingue declared in October by Capt. John Loring of H.M.S. *Bellerophon.*[63] A similar complaint had been made by Madison to Thornton, before Merry's arrival, concerning a general blockade of Martinique and Guadeloupe proclaimed by Commodore Hood to be effective from June, 1803.[64] In response to the earlier complaint transmitted through Thornton, the British Admiralty on January 5, 1804, ordered Hood and the vice-admiralty courts in the West Indies to consider a blockade as being valid only when specific ports were actually invested by a naval force, and it directed that vessels bound for such ports could be captured only if they had been previously warned to stay away.[65] It became Merry's responsibility to transmit on April 12, 1804, a copy of the January order to Madison, who expressed "great satisfaction."[66] Because of this favorable turn for the Americans, Merry was determined to seek something in return, and in August he sought Madison's intervention to prevent the arming in American ports of enemy vessels bound to ports in the possession of Britain's enemies in the East and West Indies.[67]

Although the blockade question in the West Indies was settled to the satisfaction of the Americans, the problem of excluding

American produce from British colonies under the navigation laws remained an issue. Relaxation of the navigation laws to permit the entry of American provisions and lumber was frequent, but when Lieutenant Governor Nugent of Jamaica proclaimed in November 1804 that within six months relaxation would cease, there was a very "disagreeable sensation" in the United States. The problem for Merry was complicated because news of Nugent's proclamation had been published at New York by the British consul in that city without the matter having first been referred to Merry.[68] But despite these difficulties, the government in England found it unthinkable to permit a permanent breach in the navigation system, and Merry was advised to inform the American government that the colonial governors might continue to exercise their discretion in relaxation policy.[69]

But if the Americans were disquieted by the British policy towards the American trade to the British colonies in the West Indies, the British were irritated by the American policy towards trade between Canada and the United States. In April 1804, Merry reported that he had received complaints that duties collected on British goods at Detroit and Michilimackinac were higher than those collected in the Atlantic ports. This to Merry was a violation of Article III of Jay's Treaty, which permitted freedom of commerce and navigation along the land frontier. Although the American secretary of the treasury, Albert Gallatin, denied that the Americans had violated the spirit of the treaty, Merry believed that the American intention was to prevent as far as possible the importation of British goods through Canada and the northwest. Observing that an important British interest was at stake, he urged his government to protect it in every possible way.[70]

Nearly two years later Merry was still concerned about the Canadian traders, especially the trade with the area west of the Mississippi River. That trade had been forbidden to the British by proclamation of Gen. James Wilkinson, governor of the Louisiana Territory. Both Madison and Gallatin denied that the terms of Jay's Treaty applied to the trans-Mississippi trade.[71] Despite Merry's attentiveness to British interests, no solution to the problem of Canadian trade was ever reached during his mission. The problem indeed was exacerbated by the rumor in the early summer of 1806 that British traders, particularly those connected with Hudson's Bay Company, had furnished the Indians with the means to attack American garrisons.[72] According to Merry, these rumors proved to be false and had been circulated for "land jobbing purposes."[73] The Canadian problem in all its ramifications was neither solved nor made worse because of Anthony Merry. While he faithfully defended British interests, the resolution lay, as was true of so many other Anglo-American problems, in the larger international struggle that would not be resolved until the War of 1812 was fought and the European war ended.

Merry's playing tit for tat with Madison over the blockade of the enemy islands was insignificant when compared with the blockading of whole segments of enemy coastline in Europe. On April 8, 1806, Charles James Fox, as British foreign secretary, notified the ministers of foreign powers accredited to the Court of St. James's that a blockade of the Rivers Ems, Weser, Elbe, and Trave had been declared.[74] A month later, on May 16, a blockade of the coast from the River Elbe to the port of Brest was declared.[75] On both occasions Fox instructed Merry to advise the American officials of the British action. Inevitably such action would produce a storm of protest in America, where the carrying trade to Europe would be adversely affected. Madison lost no time in informing Merry that such a blockade was illegal if it were only a paper blockade, and he pointed out that this interpretation was in keeping with the British disavowal of Commodore Hood's action in the West Indies: the same disavowal that Merry himself had transmitted to Madison in April 1804.[76]

A month after Madison's acidulous comments, Merry wrote Fox that the European blockade had "produced all that Sensation throughout the Country which is manifested immediately whenever any Thing occurs to impede the Inhabitants from enjoying their full Scope of Commercial Gain." According to Merry, the blockade was represented in America as being "a fresh Instance of what is termed that intolerable Tyranny over the Seas which is constantly exercised by the British." The government, Merry observed, had permitted the official paper, i.e., the *National Intelligencer,* to insert "as much abuse against Great Britain as ever appeared in the Public Prints of this country at the moments of the highest Irritation." Merry also made a perceptive observation when he commented that the disavowal of a distant naval officer's proclamation of a general blockade (as was done in the case of Commodore Hood) did not commit the home government to refrain from declaring a general blockade if it saw fit to do so. "Mr. Madison," Merry tartly concluded, "has put his construction on the order," i.e., the disavowal of 1804, "to establish his principle."[77]

A more explosive issue in Anglo-American maritime relations than the legitimacy of blockades was the carrying of produce from enemy colonies to Europe in American ships that broke their voyages by entering American ports. This trade was permitted by the British before 1805 under certain conditions, viz., landing the goods and paying a duty. The broken-voyage doctrine, which had been laid down by a British admiralty court in the case of the *Polly* in 1800, was overturned in the case of the *Essex* in July 1805. Wholesale captures of American shipping involved in the indirect carrying trade followed the *Essex* decision. Again Merry was placed in an awkward position, for he was not forewarned of the change in British policy. Repercussions from the captures under the *Essex* decision began to reach Merry late in the summer, while he was visiting near Philadelphia.

Writing Lord Mulgrave in September, Merry advised the foreign secretary that "a most unfavorable sensation" and "a great degree of irritation" had developed. Insurance rates, he noted, had quadrupled as a result of the captures. He also observed that the irritation in America was aggravated because the new British policy was so unexpected. Thus Merry was much surprised when he encountered Madison in Philadelphia and the secretary of state did not even mention the recent captures.[78] When he returned to Washington in October, he was astonished that when Madison finally brought the subject up, he spoke with greater moderation than Merry expected in light of the secretary's "natural irritability" and the commotion arising from the captures. To counter Madison's contention that the *Essex* doctrine was a change from earlier policy, Merry sensibly replied that the circumstances had changed, and thus a change of measures was required. Merry also suggested that His Majesty's government had probably learned that the policy of duty payments on trans-shipped cargoes in American ports was completely deceptive because they had been reduced to a mere formality. Indeed, Merry observed, it had been confessed to him that duties were often not paid at all. Merry was probably even more astonished when Madison did not react to this last charge and turned instead to a discussion of the deterioration in Spanish-American relations.[79]

This subject was calculated to arouse the interest of the British minister, who was mindful that Spain had declared war on Britain in December 1804. The secretary of state's unexpected and unaccustomed frankness, aptly described by Henry Adams as "a moderate degree of coquetry," was for the purpose of promoting more cordial relations with Britain and thereby threatening Spain and her ally France with the possibility of Anglo-American cooperation.[80]

Spanish-American relations in 1805 had reached their nadir with the failure of James Monroe's special mission to Spain earlier in the year. The most troublesome issue between the two countries was the American claim that Spanish West Florida between the Mississippi and Perdido rivers was included in the Louisiana Purchase, since that area had originally been a part of French Louisiana. Exacerbating the issue was the passage by Congress in February 1804 of the Mobile Act, which nominally made the disputed area of West Florida a customs district of the United States. Other issues concerned claims for damages arising from the plundering of American shipping by the Spanish when their allies, the French, were engaged in the Quasi-War with the United States, the condemnation of American vessels by French consuls in Spanish ports, and the suppression in 1802 of American entrepôt privileges at New Orleans by Spanish colonial officials. Moreover, there was a dispute over the location of the boundary between Louisiana and Spanish Texas. In recounting to Merry the American grievances against Spain, Madison dwelt on the "perfidious and insolent" proceedings of Juan Venture Morales and the Marqués de Casa Calva, former officials of

Spanish Louisiana who continued to reside at New Orleans after the American officials had taken over. These two caused much trouble for the new regime by encouraging opposition in West Florida, especially among land speculators, to the American claims to that region and by spreading rumors that the United States intended to exchange Louisiana for the Floridas.[81]

If Merry was jolted by being taken into Madison's confidence regarding Spanish-American relations, he must have been almost overcome when President Jefferson, his old adversary in the etiquette fracas, spoke to him with "great frankness" concerning the Spanish-American relationship. But that was not all, for the president actually lamented that despite the superiority of the British navy and the vigilance of its officers, a French naval force then harassing shipping in American waters had not been prevented from crossing the Atlantic. Moreover, the president, according to Merry, indicated some disposition to ally with Britain against France and Spain. Not only did Jefferson's conciliatory manner suggest to the astonished Merry that there was a desire for good relations with Britain despite the consequences of the *Essex* decision, but a "confidential person" assured him that Britain's new maritime policy had come at an unseasonable time and in some quarters had diverted American attention away from the trouble with Spain.[82]

But if Jefferson and Madison had been toying with the idea of cooperation with Britain against Spain, their thinking underwent a change shortly after they talked with Merry in the fall of 1805, for they learned from John Armstrong, the American minister to France, that Talleyrand had offered his good offices in behalf of the United States to prod Spain into giving up West Florida.[83] It should not be overlooked either that the administration could hardly afford to ignore the howls of anguish coming from the American shipping interest, which was feeling increasingly the effects of the *Essex* decision at the hands of the British navy. Thus Anthony Merry was not destined after all to serve as an instrument of rapprochement. On December 2, 1805, he reported to Mulgrave that anger over the detention of American vessels was increasing, and he alluded to the resolutions of grievance passed by commercial groups in Baltimore, Norfolk, and Philadelphia.

Merry also commented on another significant development, viz., that administration papers such as the *National Intelligencer* (compared by him to the French *Moniteur*) had lost sight of the grievances with Spain in expressing indignation over British maritime policy. He noted that in the *National Intelligencer* various proposals were discussed for combatting the *Essex* policy, such as the imposition of extraordinary duties on British ships and merchandise, the prohibition of American exports to British territories, and even the prohibition of all intercourse with Britain. Merry also observed that the American people were being reminded of the economic measures taken against the Crown in 1774 as well as of the economic sanctions against Britain proposed by James Madison in 1794. The British minister was also taken aback when he noted the change that had come over the secretary of state since October; by the end of 1805 Madison considered the British captures under the *Essex* decision a more urgent matter.[84]

Anxious to learn what the president would say in his forthcoming message to Congress in December, Merry detained the monthly sailing of the packet from New York to Falmouth until he could obtain a copy. Even though he had noted a change in Madison's attitude, Merry was startled that in his message the president gave priority to the *Essex* policy instead of to the troubles between Spain and the United States. In the copy he forwarded to the Foreign Office, Merry underscored the section calling on Congress to provide a remedy against "new principles . . . interpolated into the law of nations, founded neither in justice nor the usage or acknowledgment of nations."[85]

During the next four months Merry anxiously followed the debates in Congress concerning American maritime grievances and the various courses of action proposed against Britain. In his reporting of the debates, Merry noted differences of opinion among congressmen as well as differences between Congress and the administration. In his interpretation of these differences, he made certain observations that may well have influenced ministerial opinion in England. In January 1806, for example, he reported that the news of Nelson's victory at Trafalgar the preceding October had impressed the committee dealing with maritime grievances, presumably giving it pause as to whether a confrontation with the Mistress of the Seas was desirable. Merry was likewise interested in following American discussions of maritime grievances elsewhere than in Congress, such as in public speeches and in the proceedings of state legislatures. He concluded from these observations that the Spanish problem had almost been pushed aside as a result of the new animosity towards Britain.

In early January, however, Merry was of the opinion that congressional sentiment was opposed to taking extreme measures against Britain. By that time he had learned that an extraordinary mission to Britain was being contemplated. In fact this was the course finally taken, when it was decided to send William Pinkney to join James Monroe in London. Although Merry hoped that none of the retaliatory proposals would be adopted by Congress, he was fully aware that fresh causes of complaint could easily result in the passing of drastic measures. He recognized that the detention of American shipping inevitably affected a commerce in which almost all citizens, either directly or indirectly, were involved.[86] Merry was so appreciative of the situation that he wrote Adm. Sir Andrew Mitchell, in winter quarters at Bermuda, urging him to order his vessels to touch occasionally at American ports during the winter months and to maintain communications with Halifax in order that the British minister might keep the navy informed of developments in the United States.[87]

In Merry's judgment, the situation seemed to have worsened by February. On January 29 a resolution had been introduced in the House of Representatives calling for a prohibition of all imports until American grievances had been redressed. Complaints had continued to pour in, and Merry reported that the distribution of a pamphlet written by James Madison against the doctrine of the *Essex* case had influenced opinion. Yet he was also aware that those who favored moderation wanted a special mission. He understood that Jefferson himself approved that course, though there is some doubt that this was true. While Merry thought it unlikely that the non-importation measure would pass in its original form, he warned that the party spirit was so much stronger "than every Sense of the real good and wel-

fare of the country that many of the Federalists . . . who might be
guided by such a Sense are disposed to encourage rather than to
oppose the Government Party. . . ." Merry feared that if such a
measure were passed, it might bring on a war with Britain that
even some of the Federalists might support in the hope that such
a conflict would be the undoing of the administration. [88]

But by the end of February, Merry must have been somewhat
less disquieted, for after a heated discussion of maritime grievances had taken place in the House, the Senate had more
calmly taken the matter up, had put aside retaliatory measures
that had been discussed and had proposed instead the sending of
a special mission to England. Likewise, a less stringent non-
importation resolution had been introduced in the House. In his
dispatch of February 24 reporting this more favorable turn,
Merry expatiated at some length on the policy of the American
govenment. At the time he wrote, he did not know that Prime
Minister William Pitt had died on January 23 and that Foreign
Secretary Mulgrave had been succeeded by Charles James Fox,
who with Lord Grenville headed a new adminstration, the cele-
brated ministry of "All the Talents."

Merry called the attention of the British ministry to the great
fluctuations in American politics and foreign policy. He pointed
out that the Americans were activated by fear of both Britain
and France and that their strategy alternated according to whatever power in Europe appeared to be supreme at the moment.
Nevertheless he was also convinced that the Americans had a
secret desire to see Great Britain humbled and sought to take
advantage of any concessions favoring neutral trade that might
be wrested from Britain when she was in distress. Thus, according to Merry, at the time that Jefferson sent his anti-British
message to Congress in December, the Americans thought Britain was in sore straits as a result of the allied defeat at Ulm in
October. Their hopes were considerably deflated, Merry reported,
by news of Nelson's victory at Trafalgar, and they were further
dejected by news of a great victory won by the allies in December.
Ironically, however, the battle at Austerlitz to which Merry
referred had been won by Napoleon and not the allies and had
hastened the death of William Pitt. Merry was generally correct,

however, in his conclusion that American policy reflected the various shifts in the European balance-of-power struggle. He carefully called this to the attention of the British government, which, he said, should have knowledge of this fact, for the king's ministers could thus form "a pretty correct judgement" of American policy without waiting for detailed reports from America.[89]

As Merry followed the congressional debates during the winter and spring of 1805–6, he viewed with great concern the United States Treasury reports on American commercial statistics. Noting the significant extent to which American trade was being carried on with the king's enemies, Merry emphasized that this afforded "very strong proof of the propriety and necessity" of British policy contained in the *Essex* decision. Such trade, according to Merry, rendered "abortive all the exertions . . . used to deprive the enemy of those commercial resources which furnished them with the means of continuing the war." He also believed that almost all the produce of enemy colonies on the American continents, as well as in the East and West Indies, was brought to and reexported from the United States.[90] Merry's strong conviction about the wisdom of the *Essex* doctrine, however, undoubtedly caused him to misjudge egregiously American public opinion on one occasion. When James Stephen's defense of the *Essex* doctrine, which was published in England under the title *War in Disguise; or the Frauds of the Neutral Flags* in October 1805, was reprinted in the United States early in 1806, Merry advised the Foreign Office that it seemed to have a favorable effect in removing some degree of the prejudices against British maritime policy.[91] That it had any degree of favorable influence is doubtful in light of the storms raised in all quarters against Britain, even though *War in Disguise* was reprinted in Baltimore, Boston, Charleston, New York, and Philadelphia.

Merry's observations on the extent and effect of American involvement in the reexport trade expressed a deep concern for protecting vital British interest and not necessarily a spiteful hostility to the United States. It was ironical, however, that his comments on this subject would be read by Charles James Fox, who was inclined to have a somewhat higher regard for the Americans than he had for Anthony Merry.

Merry was unable to have much influence on the course of events in either England or America in the spring of 1806. Congress finally passed the Non-Importation Act on April 18, primarily in retaliation against the *Essex* doctrine. The act, prohibiting the importation of certain British manufactures, was not to become effective until November 1806. In the meantime it was hoped that the special mission consisting of James Monroe and William Pinkney might resolve Anglo-American problems through negotiation. Merry was pleased that Pinkney, a Federalist, was familiar with Britain because of his having resided in London for six years as a member of the maritime spoliations commission provided by Jay's Treaty. Pinkney, according to Merry, possessed a "moderate conciliatory disposition."[92] Yet he was also aware that Pinkney was the author of a much discussed memorial in behalf of the merchants of Baltimore against the violation of neutral rights.[93]

A few days after the adjournment of the Congress that had passed the Non-Importation Act and had approved the Monroe-Pinkney mission, Merry reported to Fox on an interview with Secretary of State James Madison. Concerning that conversation, Merry complained about the "unfriendly . . . and hostile sentiments and measures" against Great Britain, such as the Non-Importation Act, which he feared would hinder the forthcoming negotiations.[94] Merry's interpretation of these measures was that they had been based on the American conviction that Britain in her debt-ridden situation and desperate military plight could no longer afford to disregard the rights of neutral powers. As Merry saw the matter, the American pretensions were based solely on their avarice.

Reports received from Monroe, Merry believed, had caused the Americans to show friendship and every favor to France. Moreover, the French minister in Washington had intimated that Great Britain would not obtain peace with France until she accepted the principle of the freedom of the seas. In concluding this dispatch of May 4, 1806, Merry in effect admonished Fox to stand firm against American "pretensions" concerning neutral rights. In view of the party rancor and division in the United States, the weakness of government, the prevailing avarice, and the opposition to internal taxes for military preparations, Merry concluded that British resistance to these American pretentions would prevail in the end. Such resistance on the part of Britain, he predicted, would have the "Salutary Effect of commanding from this Government that respect which they have nearly lost towards Great Britain."[95] While it is impossible to say whether Merry's admonition had any effect on the negotiations that resulted in no concessions by a British ministry supposedly more sympathetic to the United States than its predecessor, he had done his duty as he saw it in counseling firmness. Moreover, his influence on British maritime policy after the fall of the government of "All the Talents" may have been greater than has been recognized, for his dispatches to the Foreign Office were available for the perusal of George Canning, the new foreign secretary, who was not disposed to be friendly to the United States.

V. Observer and Reporter

In addition to defending British national interest in such matters as maritime policy, Anthony Merry was responsible for observing the American scene and reporting on domestic politics and foreign relations of the United States. That responsibility entailed collecting and evaluating information and then transmitting it to the Foreign Office and other agencies in England, as well as to British colonial and consular officials and naval commanders in North America. Miscellaneous information pertaining to trade, ship timber, coinage, finance, political proposals, and ship movements was gleaned by the minister's observation or was delivered to him by interested persons for transmittal to England. In carrying out his duties as observer, reporter, and agent, Merry depended on contracts with American officials; conversations with private citizens and visitors to the United States; limited travel in Virginia, Maryland, and Pennsylvania; and social intercourse.

Official social functions at the British legation also facilitated the making of important contacts and the acquiring of valuable information. These functions were also a means of maintaining the dignity of the minister's position and that of his sovereign as well as of cultivating good relations with American citizens in both official and private capacities. Before Merry's arrival in the United States, Edward Thornton had advised the Foreign Office that a British minister in the new city of Washington should be able to provide extensive hospitality. Such hospitality was necessary—according to Thornton—in order to have "the most common intercourse with characters of influence," because the new capital city was so lacking in public accommodations. Thornton lamented that he himself had not been able to show "the slightest hospitality to a passing Englishman."[1]

Whether Thornton's advice was passed along to Merry or not, he and Mrs. Merry obviously considered the social role of the

British minister in Washington especially important. The size of their domestic staff, requiring two houses for its accommodation, and the dazzling accoutrements accounting for the extensive luggage of the Merrys reflected such concern. That Merry placed particular emphasis on the social aspect of diplomacy is illustrated by Foster's comment that the minister was "without any vanity but in his Table."[2]

The Merrys frequently entertained at the British legation, where they received American officials and congressmen of both parties, though sympathetic Federalists were more frequently seen. Congressman Manasseh Cutler, a guest at one of the legation dinners, described the Merry's table, the object of the minister's vanity, as "superb with plate in center, six double-branched silver candlesticks, and knives, forks, and spoons of gold in the last course." The dinner was followed by a very pleasing entertainment, with coffee served in the drawing room. A few days later, Cutler was again a guest of the Merrys for tea and cards when there were some 150 to 200 guests, including 35 members of Congress and heads of departments with their wives and daughters, gathered for refreshment and diversion while a band engaged for the occasion furnished music.[3]

Not all congressmen, alas, were as favorably impressed as Cutler. Augustus J. Foster recounts how one Kentucky congressman at Merry's elegant table declared loud enough for his hosts to hear that bad Kentucky cider was preferable to the vintage hock that he was drinking and then proceeded to spit it out behind his chair.[4] Even the eccentric John Randolph of Roanoke—with his partiality for English culture—when asked by Merry after dinner if he would take a hand at cards, replied, "No Sir, I do not know a king from a queen, or *a king from a knave*."[5] Perhaps while recalling such instances of American gaucherie in after years, the Merrys might have consoled themselves that their footman, John Sioussat, whom they left behind in America, helped improve Washington cuisine when he was hired by James Madison as chef and maître d'hôtel.[6]

Merry, despite his attention to the social role of a British minister, was not unmindful of the importance of travel in the United States for the purpose of observing the American scene.

His first travel experience in the United States from Norfolk to Georgetown in 1803, however, had caused "inward groanings" for the minister, according to his wife. But, nevertheless, a few months after his arrival in America, Merry was resolutely making plans for leaving Washington during the summer months, or or what he termed "the unhealthy season," when most of the American officials also deserted the capital. Before returning in October, he intended to visit Philadelphia and New York, in order to acquaint himself with American public opinion more than he could expect to do in the "confined" situation of Washington.[7] Unfortunately, though, Merry's plans met with several mishaps. Leaving Washington on July 6, 1804, he was detained at Baltimore for five days by the loss of his coachman, a great inconvenience, since good coachmen were hard to find.[8] When Merry reached Philadelphia in July, he was ill, and Phineas Bond, the British consul in that city, reported that he appeared to be overworked and in a "very critical state" of health.[9] Thomas Barclay, the British consul at New York, also commented on the state of Merry's health and intimated that he had apparently suffered several apoplectic seizures. According to Barclay, Merry was "very nervous, dejected, weak, and almost incapable of doing business," with his life even being in a "precarious" state.[10] Before coming to America, Merry had been under medical treatment for a "distressing disorder," which could possibly have been some disorder of the nervous system. More likely, however, the "distressing disorder" was hemorrhoids, for Merry had been referred by his physician in England to the eminent Philadelphia surgeon, Dr. Philip Syng Physick, who operated on Merry for that ailment in early October.[11]

While Philadelphia, as a center of American cultural life, would naturally attract a foreign diplomat, its medical facilities were of major interest to the Merrys in the summer and fall of 1804. Because of the nature of the surgery Merry had undergone and the condition of the roads between Philadelphia and Washington,—which together would have caused groanings more piteous than those he uttered on first reaching America,—Merry was unable to return to the capital until late December.[12] Even then his recently arrived new secretary, Augustus J. Foster, wrote that the minister was in constant alarm lest his disorder return.[13] In the following year of 1805, the Merrys returned to Philadelphia in August for medical treatment and remained until October.[14] Mrs. Merry had been ill earlier in the year, and Foster reported that she suffered greatly. During the 1805 visit to Philadelphia, an outbreak of yellow fever compelled the Merrys to seek refuge at a country tavern on the outskirts of the city.[15]

Mrs. Merry especially seemed to suffer from ill health as a result of the climate, the desertion of servants, and the incivilities of America. According to Foster, she looked ten years older than when she left England. Foster was grieved to observe the fretting and suffering of the Merrys, who were so unsuited "to bear with the horrors of a Washington residence."[16] They fled again from these horrors in the summer of 1806, their last in the United States. Merry, however, could not bring himself to go to Philadelphia, for fear of another epidemic of yellow fever, and went instead to Lancaster, Pennsylvania, where he and his wife remained from August to October.[17]

Thus the ill health of the Merrys and the need to visit Philadelphia twice for medical treatment prevented extensive travel in the United States. Yet Merry's friend Francis James Jackson exaggerated when he exclaimed that the Merrys probably never got a mile out of Washington except when on their way to Philadelphia.[18] They did visit Annapolis once on an excursion with Foster,[19] and on another occasion Merry spent some time at Mount Vernon as the guest of Supreme Court Justice Bushrod Washington, who had inherited the estate from George Washington, his uncle. In giving an account of that visit, Foster complained that the bedrooms were "miserably small" and "dreadfully hot." Moreover, feed for Merry's horses had to be procured elsewhere, because the oats and hay at Mount Vernon were too green and embarrassing consequences might have followed if the horses had been fed the provender provided. Not only did Merry, his secretary, and their horses fare poorly at Mount Vernon, but the Mount Vernon Negroes drank the liquor provided for the British minister's servants, who were obliged to buy spirits at a nearby public house.[20] Experiences away from the capital such as those that Merry had at Mount Vernon or along the road from

Washington to Philadelphia or on the way from Norfolk to Washington when he first arrived in the United States could hardly be
expected to give him a magnanimous or comprehensive understanding of the American scene.

Merry's limited acquaintance with the geography and life of
the United States was something of a handicap to him as an
interpreter of the American scene. Yet an appraisal of his effectiveness as a diplomat must be based primarily on his ability not
as an observer and reporter of American social conditions, but as
an agent of military and social intelligence. In wartime especially, the British minister would find it necessary to maintain
contact with British naval commanders in American waters.
Within a few weeks after Merry's arrival in America, Adm. Sir
Andrew Mitchell of the British North American Squadron
arranged to communicate with him through the British consuls
at New York and Norfolk.[21] Merry, however, wanted to maintain
even closer communication with Mitchell and requested the
admiral to order his captains to enter American ports frequently,
to acquaint him of their arrival, and to wait for an answer. Moreover, Merry desired that the captains should be allowed to proceed directly to England if he had dispatches that he did not
think should wait for the regular mail packets between New York
and Falmouth.[22] Although Mitchell could not comply with the
last part of Merry's request because of his limited force, Merry
did maintain close contact with the squadron during his stay in
America.[23] Merry often communicated with the commanding
officer of the North American Squadron as well as with the Foreign Office concerning the activities of French warships in American ports, such as their arrival, refitting, and departure.[24] Movements of British men-of-war were also reported by Merry, along
with requests for naval protection off certain parts of the American coast where British shipping was being harassed by French
and Spanish marauders.[25]

On occasion Merry transmitted important naval information
to Britain that did not pertain only to the movements of ships. In
a dispatch of April 1804, he reported that a United States naval
force being fitted for service in the Mediterranean had incurred
delays and great expense because of the "backward and impov-

erished" state of the Washington navy yard and the shortage of matériel and personnel.[26] In accordance with a directive from the Foreign Office, Merry reported to the Admiralty on the availability and suitability of live-oak ship timber on the coast of South Carolina, after making inquiries through the British consuls at Charleston and Norfolk.[27] In August 1806, Merry apprised the Foreign Office that "every exertion" was being made in various American ports to complete the building of gunboats, a large number of which would be stationed at New York. Although he did not elaborate on this item of naval intelligence, he must have recognized that the Americans were taking measures for self-defense, especially against the highhanded acts of British cruisers off New York.[28]

Among other routine matters that Merry handled with promptness and efficiency was arranging for the payment of money awarded Britain by the Convention of 1802, settling the claims of British creditors against American citizens.[29] As befitted a "clockwork" minister who was a merchant's son, Merry faithfully complied with requests from the British Board of Trade for statistics on the imports and exports of the United States. Some of the information he sent back may well have led to the 1805 change in British policy towards the reexport trade of the United States in the produce of enemy colonies, which was set forth in the case of the *Essex*. With his meticulous clerical habits, Merry undoubtedly reveled in sending to England copies of the American treasury reports, as well as numerous statistics concerning the army, navy, population, and shipping tonnage of the United States.[30] He was fully aware of the significance of the expedition of exploration in the trans-Mississippi West by Meriwether Lewis and William Clark during 1804–6. In almost his last dispatch from America, he noted the safe return of Lewis and Clark to St. Louis and carefully recorded that they had descended the Columbia River to the Pacific and had ascertained that its mouth was 3,600 miles from that of the Missouri and 4,400 miles from Washington.[31]

While information gathered by a diplomat abroad pertaining to exploration, trade statistics, military intelligence, and intrigue may be useful, a greater test of acumen in diplomacy involves the ability to ferret out and interpret significant political trends in the country to which the diplomat is accredited. How did Merry, who has so often been criticized as a second-rate diplomat, measure up to the test? As might be expected, he was assiduous in sending back to England his comments on the political scene at Washington. He frequently enclosed in his dispatches numerous clippings from newspapers and pamphlets published in the United States. Yet his querulous temperament, restricted travel, and a tendency to associate mainly with Federalists limited his perspective.

Merry, however, was able to size up quickly and shrewdly some American political situations. He had been in the United States but a few weeks when he observed that passage of the Twelfth Amendment to the United States Constitution, requiring members of the electoral college to distinguish on their ballots the persons voted for as president and as vice-president, had been accomplished by means of "art and intrigue." In this comment he was referring to the astuteness of Albert Gallatin and DeWitt Clinton in reminding the wavering Republicans that without the amendment the Federalists might support any Republican vice-presidential candidate for the presidency, even Aaron Burr—a subtle reminder that the disaster so narrowly averted in 1800 might yet still occur if they did not fall in line and vote for the amendment. [32]

Merry's observation of the American political struggle reflected both shrewdness and political bias. In reporting on the caucus of the supporters of the administration just before Congress adjourned in March 1804, he declared that however "preposterous" such a proceeding might appear, it was especially necessary in a presidential campaign, when so many had the right to vote for presidential electors. He also correctly observed that the Federalist Party, with its elitist bias against appealing to the populace, would be at a disadvantage. Merry sided with the Federalists in their bitterness over the impeachment of Judge John Pickering and Justice Samuel Chase in 1804 and concluded that if the political principles of the two jurists had conformed to those of the administration, scarcely any censure would have ensued. The attempt to remove the two jurists, according to Merry, stemmed from the desire of the administration to bring the judiciary completely under its control.[33]

Sympathizing with a Federalist proposal to move the meeting place of Congress, he observed that the capital would remain in Washington because of the great influence of the Virginians, as well as the great expense of making a change.[34] The "Democratic Party," he said, was "unfortunately" in the ascendancy in the spring of 1804, and only the election of Burr as governor of New York might create difficulty for that party, though Merry saw no hope of success in that quarter.[35] Indeed, the administration party seemed to be extending itself in every quarter as the summer of 1804 approached. To Merry and his Federalist friends it seemed that this trend would continue until there was so much injustice and disorder that a revolt would occur.[36] Almost any semblance of Federalist opposition had ceased, he wrote on July 2, and a few days later, in noting the death of Hamilton—"one of the great political characters" of the United States—he observed that the Jefferson administration would acquire considerable strength from the removal of Hamilton's opposition.[37] But despite the predominant position of the president's party in 1804, Merry did not believe that Jefferson would risk any diminution of his popularity in an election year by a war with Spain for West Florida, even though the administration was eager to obtain that area.[38]

After the triumphant reelection of Jefferson in November 1804 and the election of George Clinton as vice-president in place of Aaron Burr, Merry was surprised by what appeared to be the restoration of friendly relations between Jefferson and Burr. He failed to understand the political reasons that made it expedient for Jefferson to court the favor of Burr, who would preside over the Chase impeachment trial in the winter of 1804–5 during his last months as vice-president. Merry, however, freely admitted that the Federalists were disposed to believe the worst always of Jefferson. Some, he said, even believed that Jefferson was so pleased to have Hamilton out of the way that he would overlook any suspicions that he might previously have had of Burr. Implying that he did not necessarily believe this, Merry was mystified that Burr, with so many talents and so much influence, still would accept Jefferson's "system of harmony" and suggested that Burr might be seeking protection against prosecution for the death of Hamilton.[39]

After the reelection of Jefferson, Merry observed the factionalism that began to appear among the victorious Republicans. He was particularly aware of Republican factionalism in Pennsylvania from his observations during his lengthy visits to Philadelphia for medical treatment in 1804 and 1805. In that state the factional struggle was between the Constitutionalists—who included Albert Gallatin, Governor Thomas McKean, George Logan, and Alexander James Dallas—and the "violent Democrats," such as Michael Leib and William Duane, who wanted to reconstitute the Pennsylvania judiciary. The moderate Constitutionalists, according to Merry, viewed the position of the Democrats as being "completely subversive" of the principles upon which the Constitution was grounded and were willing to cooperate with the Federalists in order to remove the Speaker of the Pennsylvania Assembly, who favored the "Jacobins."[40] In his analysis of party schisms both in Pennsylvania and New York, Merry alluded to the party spirit that raged so strongly among the individuals of all classes as to be almost their sole preoccupation. This was a sound observation of the burgeoning American democracy. Merry was also correct in reporting that President Jefferson considered it expedient to side with the moderates or Constitutionalists in Pennsylvania.[41] He was, however, incorrect in assuming that the Constitutionalists were a genuine third party—a term, incidentally, that he was one of the first to use in describing American politics.

In 1804 and early 1805, Merry was mainly concerned with observing Republican schisms in Pennsylvania and New York, but in 1806 he began to notice the developing schism at the national level of the party. When the House of Representatives was debating the state of Spanish-American affairs in February 1806 behind closed doors, Merry correctly assumed that the debate was kept from the public because of the "severe observations" made on the president's conduct of foreign policy. These "severe observations" to which Merry alluded were the beginning of the break between Jefferson and John Randolph of Roanoke, caustic critic of the president's policy towards West Florida.[42] To

Merry and other Englishmen this rupture within the administration portended a return of the Federalists to power.[43] Randolph's printed diatribe against Jefferson would, in Merry's view, inevitably result in the alienation of some members of the President's party from the administration.[44]

Merry's interpretation of the American political scene was often sound, but because it was sometimes flawed, he gave unfortunate advice to the Foreign Office regarding the Anglo-American relationship. In May 1806, he advised the adoption of a sterner policy towards the Americans in order to command from them the respect for Great Britain that they had nearly lost. Among his reasons for thinking that the Americans would be compelled to yield to a sterner policy was the acrimonious party situation, leading—he thought—to a weakness of government. Contributing further to such weakness was the American intolerance of internal taxes stemming from "the predominant passion of avarice" in the United States, which caused the Americans to deny their government the necessary means for providing defense.[45] Until the end of his mission, Merry harped on the schisms in the Republican party. As he saw it, those schisms weakened considerably the influence of the administration. The publication in August 1806 of John Randolph's *Decius* letters attacking the underhanded proceedings of the administration in foreign policy seemed to confirm Merry's impression.[46] At the same time, however, he analyzed correctly the effect of Randolph's blast on the presidential aspirations of James Monroe, who was favored by Randolph over James Madison. When requested by the Foreign Office to comment on Monroe's prospects, Merry replied that Madison's influence was greater as a result of Randolph's attack.[47] But he was quite incorrect in thinking that there was some indication of Jefferson's desire to remain in office for a third term, though the president was being urged to do that by some of his followers.

In reporting on the American political scene, Merry not only noted the struggle between and within the political parties but was also alert to symptoms of unrest that might have presaged the breakup of the Federal union. He believed and hoped, as did most Englishmen of the time, that the American union was too frail a fabric to last. Thus he observed with more than a detached interest the schemes of the New England disunionists and Aaron Burr. He also followed with considerable interest the discontent that arose among the Creoles of Louisiana when they did not obtain the constitutional guarantees they had been led to expect under the 1803 purchase treaty. Merry perhaps even took delight in concluding that because of the difficulties of governing the newly acquired area, the United States intended to keep Louisiana in some semblance of colonial status as long as possible.[48] Difficulties leading to the Creole dissatisfaction included the dissimilarity of their manners, customs, and language from those of the Americans. According to Merry, the situation was complicated by the "influx of wild adventurers and enterprising speculators from all parts of the United States, especially from the back settlements where the Inhabitants knew of no restraint." The situation was such that an explosion might well occur, the British minister reported.[49]

While Merry was reporting on the Louisiana situation in March of 1804, he was inclined because of the etiquette quarrel to listen sympathetically to his fellow sufferer Yrujo, the Spanish minister. To Merry the Spaniard expressed his resentment over the retrocession of Louisiana to France and its subsequent sale to the United States.[50] Moreover, Yrujo was outraged by the American claim that West Florida was included in the Louisiana Purchase, and he was apprehensive that the United States might employ force to obtain both East and West Florida. Yrujo wondered whether the British government might be interested in lending its aid in an indirect way to thwarting American expansion in the Gulf region. In reporting to the Foreign Office his conversations with Yrujo, Merry—while ostensibly citing the don—emphasized his own comprehension of the Gulf region's strategic importance to Britain. In effect he pointed out that if some way could be devised to minimize the value of New Orleans to the United States and to prevent the Americans from acquiring other outlets to the Gulf, Western loyalties to the republic might be weakened and British commercial and political influence in the West might be promoted.

Merry also pointed out that possession of the Floridas would give the United States considerable strategic advantage over the British West Indies and the trade passing through the Strait of the Bahamas. What form indirect aid to Spain from Britain against the United States might take was not spelled out by either Yrujo or the British minister. Merry may have hinted at the possibility of fomenting trouble for the United States at New Orleans by stirring up the Creoles when he wrote of their animosity to the American officials. He did, however, suggest that British influence in the West be strengthened by the widespread distribution of British goods there and by sending agents to New Orleans to buy American produce. But despite these somewhat vague and tentative suggestions, Merry only listened sympathetically to Yrujo's recital of Spanish grievances against the United States. He was only a listener and a suggestive reporter to his government, not a promoter on the spot against his host country.

The discussions in Congress pertaining to Louisiana were closely followed by Merry. He sent home a description of the territorial government and observed that the legislative council would probably be composed of Americans, to the exclusion of the old inhabitants.[51] Despite rumors of disorder and dissatisfaction in the newly acquired territory, Merry noted that Madison assured him that American authority would prevail.[52] The discontent at New Orleans mentioned by Merry arose from the absence of elective offices in the territorial government and the failure to provide for popular participation in the legislative council. The questioning of land titles by the new regime, the levying of direct taxes whereas only tariff duties had been previously collected, and the use of English as the official language also antagonized the Creoles. In addition there was a demand for immediate statehood and for a continuation of the slave trade, which had been forbidden by Congress. The discontent, some of which had been deliberately stirred up by ambitious newcomers from other parts of the United States, led to the calling of a public meeting at New Orleans in July 1804, which drew up remonstrances to be presented to Congress by deputies sent to Washington.[53]

In view of these developments, Merry was justified in doubting Madison's optimism when he read the spirited remonstrances against the Louisiana government act. Copies of these remonstrances were sent on to London with the observation that if there were no concessions to the Creoles, they might take steps towards independence.[54] In March 1805, Merry reported the arrival of three deputies from Louisiana, who urged the government of the United States to honor the terms of the 1803 treaty of cession, which had stipulated that the inhabitants of Louisiana should be incorporated into the Union as soon as possible and admitted to all the rights and privileges of American citizens. Although these deputies avoided contacts with the agents of other governments in Washington, they expressed dissatisfaction with the official reception they received and left the capital declaring they must seek redress elesewhere.[55]

Merry's comments on the unrest in Louisiana and his reports on the state of political parties, while superficially accurate, very likely gave the British government a somewhat distorted picture of the instability of American government and politics. Such distortion might have contributed to some of the unfortunate decisions in formulating British policy towards the United States during the years preceding the War of 1812. Likewise, Merry's interpretation of American foreign policy, both towards Britain and other countries, affected the Anglo-American relationship. The first indication that Merry's interpretation might have had a detrimental influence was in connection with the British rejection of the King-Hawkesbury Convention of 1803.

That convention had been negotiated in London by Rufus King, the American minister, and by Lord Hawkesbury, the British foreign secretary, and pertained to the Northeastern and Northwestern boundaries of the United States. The convention was negotiated without knowledge of the Louisiana Purchase, and the United States Senate subsequently rejected Article V, delimiting the Northwest boundary between the Lake of the Woods and the Mississippi River, for fear that in some way it might jeopardize the new territorial claims under the Louisiana Purchase.[56] In a dispatch of December 6, 1803, Merry expressed concern over the delay and reported that the Americans were afraid of a possible conflict with the newly acquired rights in Louisiana.

He also expressed suspicion that some individuals in the United States sought to encroach on British rights. Undoubtedly Merry's suspicions were increased when Madison gave no satisfactory explanation for the delay and went so far as to say that the boundary of Louisiana should be agreed upon before the convention was approved.[57]

As weeks passed, Merry became increasingly suspicious of American motives, and on January 30, 1804, he reported that Madison sought to avoid all conversation on the matter.[58] Merry also stated that he had learned from friendly senators, presumably Timothy Pickering and other disgruntled Federalists, that the Senate would probably approve the convention with the exception of Article V, and on February 9 that was what the Senate did. Shortly thereafter Merry charged that the rejection of Article V was for the purpose of depriving Great Britain of her right to navigate the Mississippi under the Treaty of Paris of 1783, when it was believed that the source of that river was in Canada. Merry recognized that the rejection of Article V was a sore point with many New Englanders, because they feared that it might prevent the acceptance by Britain of the other articles pertaining to the Northeastern boundary, with which they were much more concerned.

According to Merry, the rejection of the amended treaty by Britain would cause the New Englanders to go forward with their plans for disunion.[59] To what extent Merry's report on the threat to British rights of navigation on the Mississippi and on the possibility of promoting New England separatism influenced the British government's rejection of the emasculated convention cannot be determined.[60] While it is reasonable to assume that Merry's interpretation did have some effect, it is more likely that Lord Harrowby, who in May became foreign secretary in the new and more aggressive ministry of William Pitt, rejected the amended treaty more because of annoyance with American presumption than because of Merry's representations. Yet Merry cannot be faulted for being mindful of British interest as he understood it, especially since his only instructions concerning the 1803 Convention anticipated that the convention, as framed in London, would have been ratified by the United States prior to his arrival in America.[61]

When Merry's first instructions were prepared in the fall of 1803, the Foreign Office was much more concerned with the state of American relations with France and Spain than with the King-Hawkesbury Convention. Thus Merry throughout his mission to America paid particular attention to American relations with those two countries and to their impingement on Anglo-American relations. One of his first duties after arriving at Washington was to protest against an unfortunately worded memorial to the French government by Robert Livingston, the American minister to France, concerning Spain's retrocession of Louisiana to France. In that memorial Livingston had commented that both France and the United States had a joint interest in resisting the "maritime tyranny" of Great Britain. Published in an American newspaper in 1803, Livingston's statement was regarded by the British as "so hostile and offensive" that it could not be ignored.[62] When Merry broached the subject to Madison, however, the secretary of state readily acknowledged the impropriety of Livingston's statement, which he deemed unauthorized and which he highly disapproved.[63]

The triangular relationship between France, Spain, and the United States—especially in matters pertaining to Louisiana and West Florida, which the Americans claimed to be a part of Louisiana—continued to concern Merry. That triangular relationship, moreover, was particularly important for Merry to watch when Britain and France were at war. Although the etiquette controversy naturally drew Merry and Yrujo together, President Jefferson attributed the intimacy of the two ministers to their expectation of war between France and Spain. If Spain were a potential British ally, Merry then would have a significant interest in Spanish-American relations, especially if the United States indicated any intention of annexing Spanish West Florida on the grounds that it had been included in the Louisiana Purchase.

In March 1804, Merry reported that French assistance would be given the United States in obtaining West Florida and that the Americans also desired East Florida. Although the Spanish minister was doubtful that anything would come of this, both he and Merry were jolted when the Mobile Act was passed in February 1804, incorporating West Florida as a customs district of the United States. This act, Merry reported, led to a very strong and justified remonstance to the United States by Yrujo, who furnished the British minister with a copy in order to keep him informed of the situation.[64] Merry was concerned not only because of the implications for a potential British ally but because of the interests of British landowners in West Florida. Madison assured him, however, that the American government would take these claims into account, and Merry thought that there was no reason to doubt the friendly disposition of the Americans on this point.[65] But despite this assurance regarding the claims of British subjects, Merry remained aware of how eager the Americans were to obtain West Florida. Yet he was correct in believing that the administration did not desire a war with Spain, and this was demonstrated by Jefferson's innocuous interpretation of the Mobile Act in a proclamation of May 20, 1804. Merry's explanation for Jefferson's restraint was that in view of the approaching presidential election, the president did not wish to jeopardize his popularity.[66]

American designs on West Florida continued in 1804 and 1805 through maneuvers in diplomacy, such as seeking the good offices of France with Spain and sending James Monroe to negotiate directly with Spain. In March 1805, Merry gleaned from a conversation with Jefferson that the president did not expect any help from France in obtaining West Florida.[67] Indeed, Merry was most astonished a few months later when Jefferson frankly divulged to him the unsatisfactory state of American relations with both France and Spain. Merry correctly interpreted his being taken into Jefferson's confidence as a move by the President to promote good relations with Britain.[68] By the end of the summer of 1805, Merry knew that the negotiations in Spain had failed and that Monroe had returned to London.[69] In November, Jefferson again talked frankly with Merry concerning Spanish-American affairs and remarked that in event of hostilities, both East and West Florida might be conquered. Merry's appraisal of the situation was perceptive, for he concluded that any adjustment of Spanish-American relations would depend on actions and events in Europe.[70] He did not know, of course, that in September John Armstrong, the American minister to France, had written Madison that Talleyrand had intimated a willingness to make available the good offices of France in negotiations with Spain.[71] But even without that knowledge, Merry probably perceived that in the wake of the widespread captures of American shipping under the *Essex* decision, the idea of Anglo-American cooperation toyed with by Jefferson was no longer viable.

Merry was well aware of the bitter debates in Congress concerning Spanish-American relations during the winter of 1805–6. Because many of the debates were secret, Merry—undoubtedly with the prompting of his Federalist acquaintances—concluded that the debates were kept from the public because of the aspersions on the way the president had handled the situation. Criticism centered on the president's secret message requesting the appropriation of $2,000,000 to facilitate negotiations for West Florida, ostensibly with Spain but also covertly with France.[72]

While the congressional debates on foreign policy were proceeding, Merry on March 19, 1806, sent a lengthy dispatch to Lord Mulgrave on the state of American affairs. In this dispatch, containing one of his more perceptive appraisals, Merry displayed a better grasp of the international situtation than he has usually been credited with having. In the same dispatch he expressed an interesting, if somewhat erroneous, view of Jefferson. He referred to the warlike sentiments of the president's December message to Congress but correctly observed that the president did not really want war with either Spain or Britain. Demonstrating that he neither understood Jefferson nor the workings of the American system, however, Merry explained the president's action as an attempt to court popularity by avoiding the charge of timidity and by leaving the matter up to Congress while he "artfully disengaged himself from all odium and Responsibility. . . ."[73]

By the time he wrote his dispatch of March 19, Merry had obtained, apparently through his Federalist connections, some inkling of John Armstrong's dispatch to Madison of the preceding September. It was Merry's understanding that the United

States had no claim to West Florida. Moreover, according to Armstrong, France would come to the aid of the Spanish if the United States should declare war on Spain. Obviously Merry did not understand that what might have seemed a threat was also a proffer of French good offices for a price. Merry was wrong about Armstrong's September dispatch being the document requested by the Senate on January 22, 1806, from President Jefferson.[74] The dispatch actually requested was the one sent by James Monroe on October 18, 1805, dealing primarily with British seizures of American shipping, in which Monroe had recommended that the United States threaten France, Spain, and Britain with war.[75] But even though his information was garbled in part, Merry had been able to learn a great deal about the secret discussions in Congress.

The British minister perceived that negotiations with Spain would be renewed and that an effort would be made to mollify France even if such a move should disrupt Anglo-American relations. Thus Merry concluded that the resolution introduced in the House of Representatives on February 10 barring certain British imports, which became the basis of the Non-Importation Act of April 18, 1806, was passed to gratify France and not to promote what he scornfully termed "the Rights of neutral nations, the exercise of which is so beneficial to France in the present war."[76] According to Merry, the Americans had persuaded themselves that while the measure could not be construed as a hostile measure against Britain, it would nevertheless frighten the British trading and mercantile elements into supporting the American interpretation of neutral rights. The president of the United States, therefore, would at the same time be able to gratify the French and to benefit American commerce by forcing a change in British policy. But since Jefferson was fearful of a loss of popularity if war between Britain and the United States should result, Merry urged that no concessions be made. Merry, moreover, expressed a hope that the British government not only would resist the American measures but would also reinforce the British naval squadron in American waters. Such a step, he believed, "would have the salutary effect of putting a stop at once to all the hostile proceedings" of the American government.[77]

It is doubtful that Charles James Fox in the British Foreign Office was influenced by this recommendation of gunboat diplomacy, but one might wonder if Adm. George Berkeley of *Chesapeake-Leopard* fame and Anthony Merry ever exchanged ideas. Although Merry apparently had little appreciation of American losses as a result of the *Essex* decision, it still cannot be gainsaid that he had a good understanding of the American relationship to the balance-of-power struggle. Jefferson's policy, he clearly recognized, fluctuated according to the latest intelligence received from Europe. As Merry saw it, the Napoleonic victory at Austerlitz was an inducement for the United States to conciliate France and to adopt unfriendly measures against Britain. Yet his overall evaluation of the American position in March 1806 was remarkably astute for a diplomat sometimes called a dunce. To Merry it was clearly evident that much depended upon the events of the war between the European powers and that every advantage would be taken by the United States of British misfortunes on the Continent.

But despite his astute analysis of the overall international position of the United States, Merry to the end of his stay in America persisted in thinking that Jefferson and the American government were unequivocally pro-French. Without giving the source of his information, he reported in June 1806 that word had come from Paris assuring the United States of French assistance in solving Spanish-American difficulties.[78] And he continued to interpret the Non-Importation Act as being primarily an effort to obtain the good will and assistance of France.[79] In almost his last dispatch from America he declared that "the fear of disobliging France in any respect and the inclination . . . of the United States towards that power was as strong as ever.[80]

With the publication of John Randolph's first *Decius* letter of August 15, 1806, blasting the intended use of the $2,000,000 recommended by Jefferson to facilitate negotiations with France, Merry took an even more jaundiced view of the conduct of American foreign policy. What Merry had not realized until Randolph's fulmination called it to his attention was that the funding of the appropriation would come through a continuation of the Mediterranean Fund, voted by Congress in 1804 to finance American naval operations against the Barbary pirates. Since this fund was raised by a 2½ percent ad valorem duty on imports consisting largely of British manufactures, Merry concluded that British trade would largely pay a contribution of $2,000,000 to His Majesty's enemies, viz., France and Spain.[81] This was all the more galling to Merry, since he had protested the passing of the 1804 act, which he believed was really a retaliatory act against a duty levied in England.[82] Allowing for Randolph's prejudice and for his own bias, Merry's conclusion about the source of the proposed appropriation was not altogether tortuous or fanciful.

In light of such a jaundiced view of American policy, it was not strange that until almost his last dispatch from America, Merry was carefully noting exhortations in the American press for the government not to relax in promoting measures that might force Britain to redress American grievances.[83] Merry's reports and interpretations of what he considered unfriendly American actions would inevitably have some influence on British policy, especially after the fall of the Grenville government of "All the Talents" and the return in March 1807 of a Pittite to the Foreign Office, in the person of George Canning.

VI. Plots of Disunion

In seeking to understand the American scene and to establish a
rapport with the Americans, Merry's task was made more difficult by the approaches of certain public men and private
individuals plotting a disruption of the federal union. These conspirators desired the assistance and cooperation of Britain and
importuned Merry to transmit their proposals to London. To
carry out his conventional duties as an agent of intelligence for
the British Foreign Office, Merry necessarily became involved
with the plotters. His involvement with the New England disunion movement of 1804 and with the conspiracy of Aaron Burr
consisted solely of listening to the conspirators and sending
accounts of their proposals and what he knew about their activities to the Foreign Office. Although Merry neither aided nor
abetted the conspiracies, his connection with them—have been
along with the etiquette controversy—the aspects of his American
mission that have received most attention, always unfavorable,
from American historians.

The winter of 1803–4, Merry's winter of greatest discontent
because of the controversy over etiquette, coincided with the period of despair for the Federalist political party. Federalists,
particularly those from New England, were in deepest gloom
because of Jeffersonian political success highlighted by the purchase of Louisiana. That acquisition seemed to presage permanent loss of political influence for the Northeast. In these circumstances disgruntled Federalist politicians, under the leadership
of Timothy Pickering, began to lay plans for detaching their
section of the country from the union and setting up a northeastern confederation. Since this project might be facilitated
with the blessing of Great Britain, they would naturally have
gravitated toward the disgruntled Merry. While Merry did have
frequent social contact with these Federalist gentlemen—who
enjoyed his hospitality, flattered his vanity, and nurtured his

resentment against the slights and indignities he had suffered at
the hands of the Jeffersonians—there is no evidence to suggest
that he had any part in the disunion plot other than listening and
reporting to London.

Yet distinguished American historians from Henry Adams on
have implied that somehow or other Merry was much more
involved with the New England plot than was actually the
case. Adams unequivocally asserts that "Merry was taken by
them [Timothy Pickering and Roger Griswold] into the secret
and gave them aid," but the only "aid" Adams specifically men-
tions was "the support of his official influence," which tells very
little.[1] Dumas Malone writes that Merry "relished disunionist
talk" and "looked toward an eventual separation, and as his later
action showed, was disposed to encourage it."[2] Merrill Peterson
asserts that Merry "gleefully reported the disunion plot to his
government."[3] Relishing disunion talk and gleefully reporting
and looking toward eventual separation are one thing; conspiring
with dissentient elements in a treasonable enterprise against a
host country is another. Prejudice against Merry, stemming
largely from the etiquette controversy, has colored the accounts
of his involvement with the plots of disunion. These accounts
reach something of a crescendo when Nathan Schachner repre-
sents Merry as having "visions of himself as the dominant arbiter
of American destiny," with "dreams of a spiteful revenge against
Jefferson and Madison" that "dazzled his poor wits and addled
his already scrambled mental processes."[4]

Actually Merry reported the schemes of Pickering and his
cohorts to the Foreign Office in a matter-of-fact way on March 1,
1804, in connection with the rejection of Article V of the King-
Hawkesbury Convention of 1803, pertaining to the northwestern
boundary. Because the New Englanders were most anxious to
have approval of the other provisions of the convention pertaining to the northeastern boundary, Merry pointed out that the
rejection of the amended treaty by the British government might
cause the disunionists to hasten their steps toward a separation.
Merry reported that he had learned from the disunionists that
their plans and calculations had been "seriously resolved" and that
"they naturally looked forward to Great Britain for support and

assistance." This expectation, according to Merry, made them apprehensive that administrative measures, such as the deliberate exacerbation of the impressment issue, might cause an Anglo-American rupture and take away possible support for their project. Merry, however, was realistic enough to realize that disunion talk in the early months of 1804 was only a trial balloon, being used as a check on the power of the administration. Yet he viewed the New England movement as "an Event in the internal politics of this country," which might "tend to accelerate that which is expected to take place sooner or later," i.e., disunion.[5]

Merry's last reference to the New England plot was made on May 7, 1804, when he advised the Foreign Office that an individual of New England had made a public suggestion that the eastern states should secede from the union.[6] But regardless of what Merry might have hoped would come from his reporting of the disunion movement, he made no recommendations to the Foreign Office, which never indicated the slightest interest and did not even acknowledge receiving Merry's account. Disinterest in London, however, did not disturb Merry, who—as a seasoned diplomat—knew that the Foreign Office often received without comment such accounts, which were sent only for information.

The failure of his home government to manifest any interest in the plotting of the New Englanders did not deter Merry from listening to the more specific proposals of Vice-President Aaron Burr for the cooperation of Britain against the United States. Burr had become acquainted with the British minister during Merry's first winter in Washington. Not only did the vice-president do Merry small courtesies, but he was captivated by Mrs. Merry, whose acquaintance he coveted for his daughter Theodosia. Although Burr had been approached by the New England plotters, there is no evidence that Merry knew this. It appears that Merry's first intimation of Burr's proposal came in early August of 1804, just a few weeks after Burr had fatally wounded Alexander Hamilton in the duel at Weehawken, New Jersey. Merry, who had gone to Philadelphia for medical treatment, was visited by Col. Charles Williamson, Burr's emissary. Williamson, a former British army officer and an agent for British land interests in western New York, was interested in recruiting men for a filibustering expedition against certain French and Spanish colonies in America. In 1803 Williamson had visited England for the purpose of promoting his project, and while there he became acquainted with Merry, who was on the eve of departing for America. Indeed, Williamson may have returned to America in the same frigate that brought Merry to Norfolk.[7] Not only was Merry acquainted with Williamson, but he had also received instructions from Lord Hawkesbury earlier in 1804 to assist the colonel's project in any way that he could.[8]

Thus Merry was enjoined to hear Williamson out, even though he must have been startled when he comprehended the import of the message from Burr. The vice-president through Colonel Williamson offered his assistance to Britain in any undertaking that might be contemplated. Burr's emissary emphasized Burr's willingness to aid in detaching the western states from the United States. Whether this was Burr's main interest cannot be determined, but he recognized that the British might well be interested in his offer and that that interest might be turned to his advantage in promoting other enterprises, such as expeditions against Spanish America. In Merry's account of the interview with Williamson—which was sent to the Foreign Office in cypher and marked "most secret"—no endorsement was given to Burr's proposal. The matter was quite properly left to the best judgment of the foreign secretary, who, as Merry observed, would soon have the opportunity of conferring with Williamson himself, since that officer was on the eve of returning again to England.[9] Although Merry's conduct in the matter of hearing and reporting on Burr's interest in possibly aiding the detachment of the West was correct, it should not be overlooked that the minister himself had alluded earlier in the year to the possibility of British aid for such a project. In his dispatch of March 13, 1804, Merry had reported that a "well-informed American" had just told him that western sentiment for disunion was greater than that of New England. Moreover, Merry had suggested that, by sending British agents to New Orleans to procure supplies for the West Indies and by flooding the Mississippi Valley with British manufactures from Canada, Britain could build up a connection with the West, break that section's ties with the East, and thus promote disunion.[10] None the less, the idea that this suggestion provided the original idea for Burr's conspiracy, as one authority has intimated,[11] is rather farfetched.

The British minister did refer to Burr's "profligacy of character" and to the fact that he had been "cast off as much by the Democrats as by the Federalist Party." He recognized, nevertheless, that Burr still had connections with people of influence and had great ambition and a grudge against the administration, all of which might cause him to use his talents "with fidelity to his employer." On balance, this was an accurate assessment of Burr and his situation, but Merry—in keeping with the accepted canons of the diplomatic profession of his time and perhaps also with his own indecisive nature—neither committed himself to Burr nor commended his proposal to the Foreign Office.

After the interview with Williamson at Philadelphia, Merry presumably had no further contact with Burr until March 1805, though Burr returned to Washington in late 1804 to preside over the Senate until the expiration of his term as vice-president in early March. During that month he called on Merry, after requesting a private interview. According to Merry, Burr commented on the discontent of the Louisiana inhabitants concerning the territorial policy of the United States. This discontent was reported to Burr by deputies sent to Washington from Louisiana. The unrest had already been indirectly reported to Merry from another source. In conversing with Merry, Burr observed that the Louisianians seemed determined to seek their independence, which could be effected by foreign aid and the cooperation of disgruntled westerners. To Merry it was clear that Burr expected to be the agent for bringing about the separation of Louisiana and the West from the United States, though Burr did not say so explicitly. He did, however, dwell on the preference of the westerners for assistance from Britain, which could profit commercially from a connection with the region.[12]

Burr declined to disclose to Merry the full extent of his plan, but he wished the British government to know of his thoughts and of his willingness to send a confidential agent to England for negotiation if His Majesty's government should indicate its interest through Merry. Burr did reveal, however, the extent of the aid

he hoped would be forthcoming from the British. He specified
that two or three frigates and several smaller vessels would be
required to keep New Orleans from being blockaded by a United
States naval force, since it was necessary to keep communications
open by sea. In terms of money Burr thought that about £100,000
would be required. Requesting an answer from the British government as soon as possible, Burr undertook to devise plans for
keeping Merry discreetly advised of his plans.

Merry's response to Burr's proposal of March 1805 was similar
to the way in which he had responded to the New Englanders
and to Burr's earlier proposal made through Colonel Williamson.
Augustus J. Foster declared in his notes on America that though
Merry listened to the plot and was bound to secrecy, he gave no
encouragement and even tried to convince Burr of its impracticality. According to Foster, Gen. James Wilkinson also entered
into conversation with Merry, who concluded that Wilkinson
was only trying to find out how much of the intrigue Burr had
disclosed, in order that he could report the minister's complicity
to President Jefferson. Moreover, Foster believed that the president would have probably liked nothing better than the opportunity for demanding Merry's recall, because of his intense dis-
like of the British minister as a result of the quarrel over etiquette.[13]

Foster's account, written between 1833 and 1845,[14] could have
been a deliberate attempt to conceal the involvement of Merry
and perhaps himself as well, but as he was writing of the matter
some three decades after the event, that seems unlikely. Although
Merry may well have only listened to Burr and reported the substance of the conversations to his superiors, the tenor of his dispatch of March 29, 1805, makes it improbable that he attempted
to convince Burr of the impracticality of his plans. While Merry
alluded to Burr's "known profligacy of character," he observed
that Burr possessed in a "much greater degree than any other
Individual" in the United States "all the talents, energy, intre-
pidity and firmness . . . requisite for such an enterprise" as that
proposed by him.[15]

This favorable assessment of Burr's abilities was sent to London
in a triplicated dispatch written in cypher and marked "most

secret." Owing to the capture of the British mail packet bound to Falmouth, however, the first two copies were lost, and the third copy of the March 29 dispatch did not reach the Foreign Office until October 15. The Foreign Office, however, had received on July 13 another dispatch from Merry dated April 29, in which he stated that he had received a further communication from Burr saying that he would soon send a confidential person who would reveal his plans to Merry.[16] Neither on the subject of this dispatch nor on the one of March 29 that was finally received on October 15 did the foreign secretary ever make any reply or comment in his instructions to Merry. Obviously the ministry was not interested in Burr's proposals, but there is no reason to conclude that it regarded Merry's conversations with Burr as impolitic or his transmittal of Burr's proposals to the Foreign Office as being irregular. To conclude, as Henry Adams did, that with the March interview with Burr, Merry was "launched into the full tide of conspiracy" is unwarranted, though Merry may well have hoped "to draw his government into a system of open and secret reprisals."[17]

The confidential person Burr promised to send to the British minister had made no contact with Merry by August 1805. Although he had received no direct word from him, Merry was of the opinion that Burr's enterprise was succeeding, because accounts of intrigue had begun to appear in the American press, e.g., in the *Gazette of the United States* of August 2.[18] In relating this to the Foreign Office, Merry in his dispatch of August 4 surmised that some of Burr's agents had been indiscreet and had betrayed him, or that the conspiracy had developed to such an extent that secrecy was no longer possible.[19] Considering what Merry wrote in that dispatch, there is no foundation whatever for the observation by Henry Adams that "Merry wrote a panic stricken letter, evidently supposing that the scheme was ruined by Burr's indiscretion."[20]

As the summer of 1805 ended and autumn came, Merry heard nothing more from Burr until late November, when Burr's confidential person, former-Senator Jonathan Dayton—detained until then by illness—arrived in Washington at last. Burr himself arrived on the scene two days after Dayton and to his disappointment and dismay learned from the British minister that no word concerning his request for British aid had been received from England, presumably because of the mishap to Merry's dispatch of March 29. He urged Merry to apprise London again of his proposal and requested that a fast-sailing naval vessel be sent to a southern port by the end of February 1806, if the British government should favor his proposal. Aware that complete understanding could not be reached without having a conference with British officials sent directly from England for that purpose, Burr told Merry that the final details could be worked out with officials accompanying the naval force sent to America. That force, according to Burr, should begin cruising off the mouth of the Mississippi by April 10, 1806, at the latest. The British warships would then receive word from Burr that the independence of the West had been declared. Burr estimated that, in order to assist such an enterprise, the British naval force should consist of two or three ships of the line, two or three frigates, and several smaller vessels. To underwrite the expenses of his land operations, Burr now calculated that a loan of £110,000 from Britain was required.[21]

In his dispatch of November 25 evaluating the latest conference with Burr, Merry accepted as true the report that the inhabitants of Louisiana were restless. That report was corroborated by Merry's knowledge of the Creole deputies in Washington. In his dispatch, Merry went so far as to say that if the opportunity to aid Burr were passed up, France might try to regain Louisiana and perhaps to annex Spanish Florida. Moreover, Merry believed that Burr, because of his late office, was privy to the secrets of United States policy. Thus Merry believed Burr when he told him that the Americans intended to resist the British policy of condemning the neutral carrying trade with enemy colonies. In light of this revelation, Merry might well have concluded that British support of Burr's conspiracy could frustrate American resistance to a British maritime policy that Merry deemed vital.

From his three November interviews with Burr, Merry appeared to be more favorably impressed than he had been previously. He declared that he believed in Burr's veracity and that he was persuaded of both the practicality and the utility of

Burr's proposal. According to Foster's recollection of thirty years later, Merry, in his March 1805 discussions with Burr, had tried to convince Burr of the impracticality of his plans. Conditions, however, had changed between March and November, and Merry now thought the time was opportune, since Britain had command of the seas and France could not interfere. Merry predicted that if the West and Louisiana were detached from the rest of the United States, the East would then separate from the South. Thus he reasoned that the "immense power" of the United States, which had so rapidly arisen in the western hemisphere, would be diminished. In short, Merry's dispatch of November 25 was something of an endorsement and a tentative recommendation of British support for Burr. Yet in reporting Burr's proposals to Whitehall, the circumspect Merry added to his commendation the qualifying words, "as far as I am able to judge."

Although Merry's official reports of his conversations with Burr were not examined by historians before Henry Adams, American officials at the time had some inkling of Burr's approaches to the British minister. In early December 1805, President Jefferson received an anonymous letter warning him to be aware of Burr's conversations with Merry and asserting that Burr was a British pensioner and agent.[22] Moreover, James Madison commented in 1807 that Merry had known about Burr's hopes to obtain British support for an expedition against Mexico but that the British minister had declined to commit his government.[23] Madison's comment was based on information that he and Jefferson had obtained from an interrogation of Erich Bollman, one of Burr's confederates, on January 23, 1807. Anxious to present the case of Burr in the best possible light, Bollman denied that his principal had sought to separate the West from the Union, but planned only to attack Mexico. To that end, Burr had communicated freely with Merry, who "entered warmly" into the discussions. Bollman took pains to say, however, that Merry, while espousing the plan for an expedition against Mexico, did not wish to offend the United States in any way.[24] Nonetheless, Merry's dispatches tell a different story, for Burr had convinced Merry that he sought the separation of the West from the United States, and that prospect was what interested the British minister. It has been claimed that Burr duped Merry into thinking that disunion was his object in order to obtain British money that he intended to use in financing the Mexican venture.[25] Although Merry was interested in American disunion, he may not have been completely duped by Burr, however. It is possible he recognized that the chameleon-like Burr had several irons in the fire and would seize the one that he judged could be used to his best advantage at the moment. Moreover, Merry apparently did know of Burr's interest in Mexico.[26] To say the least, Merry was not so trusting or so indiscreet as to be duped into advancing Burr any money from his legation's discretionary fund—as was Yrujo, who supplied Burr with $1,500 for the western project.[27]

Madison's conclusion that Merry had not committed the British government to Burr's proposal concerning Mexico could have applied to any part of Burr's intrigue. Merry listened to whatever Burr saw fit to tell him. He may even have been gullible enough to believe Burr, and he very likely hoped that the British government would support Burr's intrigues against the United States, but that was as far as the prudent and cautious minister dared to go. Because of their previous brushes with Merry, Jefferson and Madison were not inclined to view him in a favorable light. Yet they never indicated that they considered he had acted improperly in his role as an agent of intelligence for his government, even though they must have suspected he had listened sympathetically to proposals for promoting disunion and had transmitted them to England with his approbation.

In commenting on Merry's dispatch of November 25, 1805—in which he came nearest to endorsing Burr's proposal—historians have made much of the fact that it reached England on February 2, 1806, ten days after the death of Prime Minister William Pitt and only five days before Charles James Fox, in the Whig ministry of "All the Talents," succeeded the Tory Lord Mulgrave as foreign secretary. Henry Adams goes so far as to assert that the dispatch intended for Lord Mulgrave was probably opened by Fox, "almost the last man in England to whom Merry would have willingly shown it."[28] Although—as later developments showed—Fox may not have thought very highly of Merry, there is no evidence to suggest that Merry was aware of this or that, if he had known Fox was in the Foreign Office instead of Mulgrave when he wrote the dispatch, it would have made any difference in what he reported or recommended.

Adams and other historians, such as Thomas Perkins Abernethy, have contended that it was the death of Pitt that prevented Merry's recommendations from being adopted by the British government.[29] This presupposes a much greater influence on the ministry than Merry ever had and a greater malevolence towards the United States than the Pitt government ever intended. There had been ample opportunity since 1804 for the Pitt government to show an interest in intrigues against the United States—which had been called to its attention either by Merry or by Col. Charles Williamson, Burr's emissary to England. Problems at home, such as the impeachment of Lord Melville, the threat of French invasion, and the defeat of Britain's allies in Europe, would have continued to make support of intrigue unfeasible even if Pitt had lived and his government had remained in office.[30]

But for whatever reasons, Burr's failure to obtain British support was a heavy blow to all aspects of his conspiracy. In desperation he called again on Merry in June 1806. In this final interview with Merry, Burr anxiously inquired if any favorable word concerning his enterprise had come from England. According to Merry, Burr had then "lamented exceedingly" when he learned that no word had been received. Yet Burr continued to misrepresent the situation to his associates, such as Gen. James Wilkinson, by telling them that a British naval force would be sent to aid the enterprise.[31]

For some reason, Merry did not inform the Foreign Office of his June conference with Burr until November 2, 1806.[32] Perhaps he decided not to comment any further on Burr's proposals, since Whitehall had not indicated the slightest interest. Moreover, he might have considered that Charles James Fox at the Foreign Office would not be impressed. Still it was uncharacteristic of Merry not to have made an immediate and full report. Stung, however, by having just received word of his recall and expecting to be relieved shortly, he may have concluded either to forget the Burr business or to await further developments in America. But his departure was delayed until the winter, and by early November rumors were flying at Washington concerning Burr's operations in the West. Merry then decided to mention, even though belatedly, his meeting with Burr in June.

On November 2, in two of his last dispatches sent from Washington, Merry made his final observations on the Burr conspiracy.[33] No longer was he recommending or even hoping that His Majesty's government might aid Burr, since it was clear to him that Britain was not interested in aiding or abetting the plot. In the first dispatch, he mentioned the rumors concerning Burr's activities in the West. According to Merry, the American officials, though disturbed by the reports from the West, surmised that a filibustering expedition against Mexico was the objective of Burr, who expected hostilities between Spain and the United States. Merry reported that the adminstration at Washington did not believe the westerners would follow Burr in a movement of disunion. In his second dispatch, which was written in cypher, Merry told of his conversations of the preceding June with Burr. Disappointed that Merry had received no word concerning British aid, Burr had then said he would turn to France and Spain for assistance. Moreover, he declared that even if no aid came from those sources, his enterprise would go forward because sentiment for disunion was so prevalent in the West.

Owing to the rumors reaching Washington from the West in the fall of 1806, Merry concluded that Burr's enterprise was getting underway. He had heard that Burr's adherents were making military preparations in the West and that money from New Orleans was being circulated among the westerners to aid the disunion plot. French and Spanish assistance was also said to be forthcoming. Merry interpreted the movement of Spanish troops from Texas towards Natchitoches in Louisiana as being connected with Burr's enterprise. In relating all this to the Foreign Office Merry was perhaps implying that if the British government had only listened to him, Britain might be reaping the benefits of American disunion as France and Spain seemed to be doing. Merry expressed astonishment that the American government was apparently so uninformed as to what was taking place in the West. This lack of information he attributed to the government's having no supporters in the West zealous enough to keep it informed.

Astute though Merry was in some matters, his observations in late 1806 pertaining to support for Burr's disunion plot in the West show him at his worst as an observer of the American scene. His reports, unintentionally misleading, could have had dangerous consequences if the British government had concluded on the basis of them that the American union was on the eve of dissolution and had decided to aid Burr's plot. Merry's judgment was seriously flawed because he never perceived the reality of American nationalism and its attendant loyalties. The American government presided over by Thomas Jefferson and his colleagues had a far more realistic understanding and appreciation of Western loyalty than the recalled British minister did. In Anthony Merry, hope always seemed to spring eternal that the American union was about to disintegrate.

The day after Merry wrote his last observations concerning Burr's conspiracy, David M. Erskine was presented to President Jefferson as the new British minister to the United States. A month later it was Erskine's duty to apprise the Foreign Office of the issuance of a proclamation by President Jefferson on November 27, 1806, warning American citizens, without mention of Burr by name, of an unlawful military expedition against the dominations of Spain.[34] What Merry, on the eve of embarking for England, must have thought of this development would be interesting to know, but to the ex-minister, Burr and his schemes were no longer of official concern.

Soon after embarking for England, however, Merry may have had an opportunity to discuss the Burr conspiracy with Capt. John Poo Beresford of the British navy. Beresford, who had temporarily commanded the North American Squadron earlier in the year, was in the frigate *Cambrian* off Cape Henry in early December and probably talked with Merry when he encountered the vessel taking the former minister back to England. In a memorandum of December 13 pertaining to Burr, Beresford wrote an acount of what apparently had been either a recent conversation with Merry or a communication from him. According to Beresford; Burr had called on Merry and had solicited British aid for effecting the conquest of Mexico and the detachment of the western states and Louisiana from the United States. The memorandum also stated that East Florida would fall "an easy prey" to Britain when Burr's enterprise got underway.[35]

Except for this last observation about East Florida, Beresford's memorandum essentially contained all that Merry had already reported concerning Burr's plans as revealed to him. Merry, however, had not commented on Burr's interest in Mexico, though he had alluded in his dispatch of November 2 to the surmise of the American administration that Mexico was the conspirator's object. Beresford's memorandum reveals that Merry had learned from Burr himself that he envisaged an expedition against Mexico as well as American disunion, despite the contention by the foremost authority on the conspiracy that to Merry "not a word was said about an invasion of Mexico."[36] The observation about East Florida very likely originated with Captain Beresford, who would have had a professional interest in acquiring a naval base to the southward, away from American territorial waters. According to Yrujo, however, Merry and Burr had discussed in March 1805 the employment of British naval force against East and West Florida, which would be attached to Burr's projected state in return for commercial concessions to Britain.[37] Nevertheless, the Floridas had not entered into the Merry-Burr conversations until November 1805, and even then there had been no contemplation of the British acquisition of East Florida, as suggested by Beresford.

After his return to England, Merry once again was sought out by Aaron Burr, who wanted to use the former minister to America as an intermediary with the British government. In the summer of 1808 the ruined Burr went to England with hopes of inducing the ministry to aid him in his plans for revolutionizing Mexico. Merry, Burr thought, might be able to assist him in presenting his project to the ministry. In 1808 Merry did have easy access to the Foreign Office, where his old friend George Hammond was serving as under-secretary. Moreover, George Canning, the foreign secretary, thought highly of Merry and was employing him in 1808 as a special translator of Spanish documents for the Foreign Office.[38] When Burr arrived in July, Merry was at Herringfleet, his countryseat in Suffolk; he did not come up to London until late October and appear's to have been somewhat dilatory in responding to Burr's requests during the summer and fall.[39] He did not offer Burr the hospitality of Herringfleet—as Jeremy Bentham did at Forde Abbey, where the American spent several weeks. The best explanation for Merry's reticence is that through his cronies at the Foreign Office, he knew that aiding Burr in revolutionizing Spanish Mexico was out of the question because cooperation with Spain was vital for Britain with the Peninsular War [1808-14] getting underway during the summer and fall of 1808.[40]

On November 6 Merry finally wrote Burr that he had failed to see Canning, who was away because of illness. He reported, however, that he had talked with another person of "nearly equal authority" (presumably George Hammond) and it appeared that the Mexican proposal could never receive British support because it was "impracticable."[41] Thus Merry ended his correspondence with Burr. In this instance Merry was for Burr what he had been in America, a polite intermediary who merely transmitted a proposal to His Majesty's government. He was hardly "ever-bubbling" in his attentions and promises to Burr, as the latter's biographer has claimed.[42] Indeed, it is just possible that Merry had something to do with the government's decision to order Burr out of England in April 1809. As George Canning's friend and aide, Merry's opinion must have carried some weight, for he had some knowledge of what he once called Burr's "known profligacy of character."

VII. The End of the American Mission and Merry's Later Career

Despite their initial irritation with Merry in the controversy over etiquette, American contemporaries in early 1804 found Anthony Merry an agreeable and easy man with whom to transact official business. But as the months passed, the inevitable Anglo-American conflicts arose as a result of the European war. Particularly bothersome were the maritime disputes arising from impressment and the seizure of American ships and cargoes. It was following a correspondence with Merry concerning the impressment issue that an exasperated James Madison privately dubbed the British minister a "mere Diplomatic pettifogger."[1] Yet it does not appear that this was a final or definitive judgment. Madison's later relations with Merry seem to have been amicable and even conciliatory.

A more telling indictment of Merry came from Timothy Pickering, a Federalist critic of Jefferson's administration, who had once sympathized with Merry and had discussed with him the New England disunion project early in 1804. In 1805 however, Pickering expressed the wish that Merry "ere long" should have a successor. Although he considered that Merry was amicable and had a good disposition, Pickering complained that in his representations against the arming of American merchantmen he had demonstrated "imbecility."[2] This complaint referred to Merry's recommendation to Madison of August 31, 1804, that American ships should be denied the privilege of arming for defense against pirates and privateers because they might pass into belligerent hands at the first foreign port.[3] The choleric Pickering could not abide the thought that Yankee shipping should go undefended because of the British minister's appehensions. Two years later, after Merry had returned to England, Pickering declared that he had been "totally incompetent."[4]

Another Federalist senator, William Plumer of New Hampshire, likewise considered Merry to have been "a feeble, inefficient man" though "easy, polite, and very civil." Plumer's harsh judgment in this instance stemmed from Merry's protest against John Quincy Adams's proposed bill limiting diplomatic privileges in the United States.[5]

But the American contemporary who perhaps came nearest to holding Merry personally responsible for an increasingly antagonistic policy on the part of Britain towards the United States was none other than Thomas Jefferson. Writing to his old friend and classmate James Maury on the eve of the War of 1812, the former president blamed Merry for ending the more favorable disposition manifested towards America while Henry Addington was prime minister from 1801 to 1804 and during the short period when Charles James Fox was foreign secretary in 1806.[6] Although it is impossible to disprove the baleful influence that Merry might have had, it is equally difficult to show conclusively how Merry's ministry had done any fundamental harm to Anglo-American relations. The worst damage that Merry might have conceivably inflicted was that his dispatches could have fostered the illusion that if the Federalists regained power, a friendlier relationship with the United States would follow.

But despite the unfavorable views of American contemporaries, Merry's colleagues in the diplomatic service continued to hold him in high esteem. Augustus J. Foster may not have been an experienced diplomatist when he served under Merry in the United States, but he was an intelligent observer and cannot be disregarded. While recognizing Merry's foibles, Foster, for the good of England, was sorry to learn of his recall, because Merry "perfectly" understood the United States.[7] Although Foster's evaluation may have been overly generous, it was significant that after serving two years under "Toujours Gai," he considered that Merry not only understood the forms of diplomacy but also the problems of the Anglo-American relationship. Merry's overall grasp of that relationship and the essential soundness of his judgment are evinced in his first official dispatch sent to the Foreign Office ten days after arriving in Washington. In that dispatch he astutely assessed the significance of the maritime factor in Anglo-American relations by writing:

. . . while it is my duty to do justice to Mr. Madison's temperate and conciliatory language, I must not omit to observe that it indicated strongly a design on the part of his Government to avail themselves of the present conjuncture by persisting steadily in their demands of redress of their pretended grievances in the hope of obtaining a great respect of their flag, and of establishing a more convenient system of neutral navigation than the interests of the British Empire have hitherto allowed His Majesty to concur in.[8]

Not only did Merry shrewdly appraise the American position in many instances, but he also demonstrated considerable courage and tenacity of purpose. Despite incivility, insalubrious climate, ill health, boredom, and loss of servants, he never indicated any desire to be released from his unpleasant and difficult American assignment. Augustus J. Foster testified to the suffering endured by the Merrys in America and to Merry's determination to remain at his post. Professional pride and habit of attending to duty over many years in the diplomatic service account for Merry's perseverance. Foster also believed that Merry was determined to remain in America because the patriotic diplomat considered that he had a special obligation to stay at his post during wartime.[9] Yet another reason for Merry's desiring to stay was the considerable financial outlay he had made in order to provide Mrs. Merry and himself with the comforts and conveniences for the extended residence he had expected to have in the United States.

But it was not left to Merry to decide how long he would remain in America. A change in the British ministry following the death of William Pitt in early 1806 brought to office men who were not only unfriendly to Merry but who had a somewhat different perspective on British politics and Anglo-American relations. The new administration also had political obligations that would entail reassignments in the diplomatic service. When Charles James Fox became foreign secretary on February 7, 1806, Merry's friend George Hammond was removed as under-secretary for foreign affairs. Merry, a strong Pittite, was unacceptable

to Fox both personally and politically. Fox had been acquainted
with Merry at least since 1802, when the latter was serving as
minister ad interim in Paris. Whether Merry offended Fox in
Paris as he had offended Thomas Erskine, Fox's friend and fellow
Whig politician, is not known, but it is certain that the foreign
secretary had a poor opinion of Merry. Shortly before Fox entered
office, he assured Lady Elizabeth Foster that if he became foreign secretary, he would not leave her son Augustus in America.
When Lady Elizabeth answered that her son had been sent to
America to serve under Merry in order to be trained by him, Fox
replied that Augustus Foster was more fit to train Merry.[10]

One month after becoming foreign secretary, Fox notified
Merry that he was being recalled because of long-continued ill
health.[11] In a letter to the king recommending the recall of
Merry, Fox observed that Merry's "infirmities and other circum-
stances" made him unfit to continue in the American mission.[12]
At the same time that Merry was apprised of his recall, he was
told that Thomas Douglas, the Earl of Selkirk, would be his
successor. Selkirk, however, did not serve, because he was named
as one of the representative peers to the House of Lords from
Scotland in 1806. Appointed instead of Selkirk was David
Montagu Erskine, son of the lord chancellor in the Grenville-
Fox government. And the lord chancellor was the same Thomas
Erskine whose wrath Merry had incurred in Paris in 1802.
Erskine, indeed, had sought the American assignment for his
son even before Fox had recommended Selkirk.[13]

In view of these obligations of friendship and politics, Merry's
recall might have been expected. Moreover, it is most unlikely
that any disapproval of Merry's conversations with Aaron Burr
had anything to do with his recall, as some historians have
claimed. But it is true that Fox and the elder Erskine sought
friendlier relations with the United States. In April 1806, the
lord chancellor told Charles Abbot, Speaker of the House of
Commons, that recent judgments against neutral shipping had
been very mischievous and that Fox thought America should be
made a friend rather than an enemy.[14] Thus it is possible that
Merry, with his tenacious adherence to the navigation system
and his staunch defense of all the traditional British maritime

rights, could have been considered unacceptable by the Grenville-Fox government on grounds of policy.

Anthony Merry, who received word of his recall in early May 1806, understood that Lord Selkirk would soon arrive in the United States.[15] Mrs. Merry wrote an American friend on May 17 that she and her husband were already "packed up" and were eagerly awaiting the arrival of the new minister, who would probably reach Washington in June. She hoped that her husband would not be immediately employed, in order that she might enjoy again her "chief delight," the garden and farm at Herringfleet Hall.[16]

But if Mrs. Merry was pleased by the prospect of an early return to England, Mr. Merry was decidedly not pleased. Although he and his wife had undoubtedly been unhappy in the United States, the circumstances of his recall were mortifying. In a private letter written to Fox on June 1, Merry expressed his bitterness in a manner that was hardly in keeping with his reputation as being the gentlest of plenipotentiaries. Indeed, a biting note of sarcasm is evident when he informed Fox that the blow of his recall was felt even more severely since His Majesty had expressed approbation of his conduct without exception or qualification. Observing that he himself would have asked for a recall if ill health had impaired his efficiency, Merry declared that despite an injurious climate he had been able to perform all of his duties except for a short time in 1804. He emphasized that he had risen in the diplomatic service through merit alone and hence was not indebted to any particular "Connexion, Interest, or Influence."[17] Recognizing that his age did not warrant such an early retirement, he acidly commented that Fox would hardly consider him eligible for another assignment since he had been judged unfit for continuing in the American mission.

Merry concluded his letter of June 1 by saying that he would rely on Fox's reputation for "Justice and Liberality" to recommend a pension for his twenty-three years of diplomatic service. He also sought indemnity for the great expense he had incurred in establishing a suitable residence in Washington. According to Merry, the financial loss was a particular hardship, since he had expended his small patrimony in obtaining his first appointment in the diplomatic service and was now deprived of reaping the advantage usually "derived from long and faithful service."[18]

It is unlikely that Charles James Fox ever read Merry's bitter letter, for by the end of June Fox was in such ill health that he was incapable of attending to his own duties. Because of Fox's illness and the resulting confusion in the Foreign Office, Merry was not informed until August 8 that Erskine, and not Selkirk, would be his successor at Washington.[19] The departure of Merry's successor was also made less urgent by the arrival in June 1806 of William Pinkney in England to join James Monroe in negotiations with Britain. Compelled to await the new minister's arrival because Foster had not been named chargé d'affaires, Merry was justifiably annoyed by Erskine's delay in reaching Washington.[20] The Merrys especially wished to avoid the Atlantic crossing in winter, when passage was not only difficult to obtain but so disagreeable and dangerous that their departure might be delayed until the spring.[21]

Erskine, however, did arrive in time for Merry to leave in early December. Soon after his successor's arrival, Merry formally presented his letter of recall and took formal leave of the American officials on November 3.[22] During the remainder of the month, he busied himself with such matters as dismantling his household, disposing of his furniture (which the Erskines obligingly bought), requesting all persons having claims against him to present their bills, and procuring passage for England on the ship *Leonidas,* sailing from Alexandria to Liverpool on December 6.[23] The *Leonidas* was to have sailed earlier, but was delayed by unfavorable winds. While waiting at Alexandria for his ship to sail, Merry received, along with his passport, a friendly farewell message from Secretary of State James Madison. In view of the uncertain state of Anglo-American relations at the end of 1806, Madison was concerned lest Merry's unfriendly feelings might dispel any tendency towards conciliation on the part of Great Britain.[24] The kindly Madison, aware of Merry's mortification over his recall, might also have been a bit remorseful for his part in the unnecessary controversy over etiquette.

Merry reciprocated Madison's friendly message by courteously apprising the secretary of state of the delay in the sailing of the *Leonidas*, in order to give Madison an opportunity to add other dispatches to the packet that he had requested Merry to send to James Monroe on arriving in England.[25] But despite the courteous exchange between Merry and Madison, the reason given for Merry's delay in sailing was questioned in the American press. The *Norfolk Gazette* reported that the *Leonidas* had not been delayed by unfavorable winds but rather by Merry's desire to ascertain whether President Jefferson in his message to Congress would recommend a further suspension of the date when the Non-Importation Act would take effect. The *Gazette* even speculated that Jefferson had been apprised of Merry's object and that accounted for the president's not making any recommendation in his message of December 2.[26] That, however, was an unlikely motive, since Jefferson recommended further suspension of the act in a special message to Congress on December 3, a copy of which Merry carried with him to England.

When Merry finally sailed on December 6, he was not accompanied by Mrs. Merry, whose health did not permit her to undergo the rigors of a winter voyage. She remained in the vicinity of Alexandria for the next several months.[27] During her last months in America, she gave little encouragement to Erskine's American-born wife when she wrote, "I would say that your being an American would be an advantage in Washington were it not for that poor lady, Madame Yrujo [née Sally McKean of Philadelphia]."[28] When Mrs. Merry left New York for England in June 1807, she traveled alone, since all her servants had deserted. In commenting on her unhappy experiences in America, Augustus J. Foster ruefully observed that no man esteeming a wife should permit her to accompany him on a diplomatic assignment to America.[29] As the lonely Merry crossed the Atlantic in the midwinter, he might well have recalled his wife's unhappiness in America and thus agreed with Foster.

After an uneventful voyage Merry reached Liverpool on January 17, 1807, and with characteristic promptness notified the Foreign Office of his arrival before the *Leonidas* docked.[30] Although—unbeknown to Merry—Charles James Fox had died in the preceding September, Lord Grenville and other members of the Fox circle were still administering the king's government.

Not favorably regarded by that political faction, Merry anticipated temporary, if not permanent, unemployment. Such, however, was not to be the case, for the Grenville government fell
in March; George Canning, a fellow Pittite, became foreign
secretary, and George Hammond, Merry's old friend, again
became under-secretary.

With these connections at the Foreign Office, Merry was soon
sent on a special mission to Denmark in the fall of 1807 for the
purpose of conciliating the Danes after the seizure of their fleet
by the British.[31] Lord Whitworth, a former British ambassador
to Paris who had followed Merry as minister ad interim in 1802,
recommended him to Canning as being especially well qualified
for the Danish mission.[32] But Lord Malmesbury, another experienced diplomatist who had thought well of Merry in the past,
indicated some misgiving about the appointment by saying that
while Merry was "very worthy" he was, nevertheless, a very
"nervous man."[33] Merry's secretary for the Danish mission was
Stratford Canning, cousin of the foreign secretary. George
Canning particularly wanted the young man to serve under a
diplomat with Merry's experience and tact. In his memoirs
Stratford Canning described Merry as having "the gentle manners of the gentlest of plenipotentiaries." Thus both Stratford
Canning and Augustus J. Foster, two distinguished diplomatists
of the nineteenth century, served as secretary to Merry in order
to be trained by him for the diplomatic service. Moreover, both
men also subsequently served as British minister to the United
States, Foster from 1811 to 1812 and Canning from 1820 to 1823.

Stratford Canning's description of Merry's encounter with the
king and queen of Sweden at Helsingborg, while awaiting admit-
tance to Denmark, has a touch of humor but is also revealing of
Merry's demeanor. On the morning of his meeting with the
Swedish royal couple, Merry had undergone a surgical operation
on his finger. As a result he had been unable to shave himself and
was thus forced to greet Their Majesties with an unkempt
appearance and his arm in a handkerchief. But determined at
all times to observe the proprieties of diplomatic etiquette, the
gentle "Toujours Gai" nevertheless managed to give a few awkward bows.[34]

The mission to Denmark was a complete failure, for the Danes refused even to give Merry permission to enter their country, and he returned to England in November. George Canning, however, continued to make use of his knowledge and experience and during 1808 regularly sent him Spanish documents to translate, because he did not trust a Grenvillite who remained on his staff in the Foreign Office.[35] There was, however, one more foreign assignment for Merry before his final retirement. In November 1808 he was named minister to Sweden, where—accompanied again by Augustus J. Foster as his secretary—he served until April 1809.[36] For his service in Sweden "under circumstances of so extraordinary and difficult a nature," the king through Canning expressed approval of Merry's conduct.[37] Thereafter Merry received no further assignments, and when George Canning and George Hammond left the Foreign Office in October 1809, he was without influential friends in the ministry.

Although for his long service Merry received a pension and the customary gift of gold plate, he did not, at least in the beginning, accept retirement in his fifty-third year with equanimity, and he complained that his letters to the Foreign Office went unanswered. His young friend George Jackson was sympathetic with Merry, who had once been "so well informed," but he later observed that despite his being cut off from the Foreign Office, Merry whenever he was in London contrived "by some means or other to ferret out most things" and sifted them "to the bottom." Merry especially regretted not having ready access to the Foreign Office because he sought information that might have been helpful to his former colleague, Francis James Jackson, when the latter was named British minister to the United States.[38] In view of Merry's close association with George Canning, George Hammond, and Francis James Jackson during the years 1807, 1808, and 1809, there was a strong possibility that the hostility of those officials towards the United States was influenced in some measure by Merry's recollection of his unhappy years in America.

In retirement after 1809, Merry settled down to the quiet life of a country gentleman at Herringfleet Hall in Suffolk, where he and Mrs. Merry maintained their permanent residence. The Hall, which had been built by Mrs. Merry's first husband, was a typical Georgian countryseat surrounded by park land, some six miles from Lowestoft.[39] Merry's new status as a country gentleman was evidenced by his acquisition of a family coat of arms and by his being named a justice of the peace, a dignity that, it was remarked, increased his wife's sense of importance at the neighboring town of Great Yarmouth. Squire Merry, the City wine merchant's son, had at last found an agreeable and permanent residence. When George Jackson met him in 1812 at Bath, where Mrs. Merry—bored by the quietness of Herringfleet Hall— had dragged him to take the waters, Merry indicated that he was anxious to return to his fireside in order to enjoy his papers and political pamphlets.[40]

The pleasant years at Herringfleet Hall were not to last, however, for Mrs. Merry died in 1824, and the estate reverted to John Francis Leathes, nephew of her first husband. Until the last, this "fine woman"—as Augustus J. Foster and Thomas Moore had described her—lived in a style becoming the gentry, a station

HERRINGFLEET HALL

Squire Merry's countryseat in Suffolk from 1803 to 1824.
(Photograph by the Rev. Dr. Edward C. Brooks.)

that she could rightfully claim, if not by inheritance, then by virtue of her first marriage, her long association with the gentry, and her own cultural attainments. In her will she stipulated that her funeral be "without parade" and that her corpse be carried to the church by her own workmen. She was buried in the ancient parish church of St. Margaret's at Herringfleet, where a mural table records that she was the widow of John Leathes, Esq., and was survived by her second husband, Anthony Merry, Esq. Among her bequests were the beloved botanical books and an endowment for paying £20 annually to maintain a school for the poor children of Herringfleet Parish. She also provided that Anthony Merry was to be reimbursed for all of the improvements he had made at Herringfleet Hall.[41] Merry remained on good terms with the new squire of Herringfleet, and in his own will he left John Francis Leathes a gold snuffbox and the portrait of Mrs. Merry painted in 1805 by Gilbert Stuart at Washington.[42]

After leaving Herringfleet, Merry established his residence at Dedham House, just outside the village of Dedham in Essex.[43] There he spent the last decade of his life in the company of his sister Sukey, an aged spinster. The old diplomat must have sometimes seen John Constable, a native of the region, who often returned during the 1820s to paint the familiar scenes of beautiful Dedham Vale. Many years after Merry's death, he was still remembered in the village of Dedham as being "a diplomat from head to foot, a ceremonious, polite, highly refined looking old gentleman . . . walking about with the most impenetrable face possible."[44]

When Anthony Merry died on June 14, 1835, his not inconsiderable estate was valued at £35,000. In his will he made bequests to his sister, two godsons, various relatives and friends (including several members of the Leathes family), and his servants.[45] Among the personal possessions that he bequeathed were a snuffbox bearing the portrait of Charles IV of Spain and three medals commemorating that monarch's coronation, which Merry had witnessed in 1788. These mementoes went to George Hammond as tokens of Merry's grateful remembrance of that official's kindness while Hammond was under-secretary for for-

THE PARISH CHURCH OF ST. MARY THE VIRGIN
Dedham, Essex

A tablet to the memory of Anthony Merry, Esq., is on the wall of the
north aisle, near the spot where he is buried in the parish church.
(Photograph by Pauline Domingos Lester.)

eign affairs.[46] These were small objects, but they symbolized a
chapter in Merry's long career in the British diplomatic service.
His old friend Hammond, who had also once served as British
minister to the United States, would appreciate them as remind-
ers of a colleague's service in Spain, a service both diplomats very
likely considered more important than their assignment in
America.

Merry did not foresee that Britain and Spain would become
lesser powers than the country where he had served George III
with such unhappiness and vexation from 1803 to 1806. Nor did
he foresee that posterity would remember him chiefly, though
dimly, because of that chapter in his almost forgotten life.
Anthony Merry lies buried near the pew that he occupied in the
stately Dedham parish church of St. Mary the Virgin, erected

in the year Christopher Columbus discovered America. The inscription on the mural tablet to the memory of Anthony Merry, Esq., in Dedham church records nothing of his long and honorable career in the British diplomatic service. Yet Merry, an English gentleman of the old school, would have approved the tablet that was put up. He might well have thought that visitors to Dedham church in the years to come would be much more impressed by such badges of gentility as the title of esquire and the emblazoned Merry coat of arms than by any mention of his diplomatic career, creditable though it may have been.

Notes
Bibliography
Index

Abbreviations Used in the Notes

Adm. Admiralty Office Papers in Public Record Office, London

FO   Foreign Office Papers in Public Record Office, London

LC   Library of Congress Manuscript Collections in Division of Manuscripts, Library of Congress, Washington

SDR State Department Records in US National Archives, Washington

Notes

Introduction

1. Henry Adams, *History of the United States during the Administrations of Thomas Jefferson and James Madison*, 3:99.
2. Edward Channing, *The Jeffersonian System*, p. 178.
3. John Franklin Jameson, "The Approach to Diplomatic History by the Correspondence of the Early British Ministers to the United States," unpublished lecture, John Franklin Jameson Papers, LC.
4. Claude G. Bowers, *Jefferson in Power*, p. 32.
5. Nathan Schachner, *Aaron Burr*, p. 285.
6. Richard Beale Davis, "Introduction" to Sir Augustus John Foster, *Jeffersonian America*, p. xi.
7. Bradford Perkins, *The First Rapprochement*, p. 182.
8. Marshall Smelser, *The Democratic Republic, 1801–1815*, pp. 145, 201.
9. Dumas Malone, *Jefferson the President: First Term, 1801–1805*, p. 384.
10. John Franklin Jameson to James D. Milner, Sept. 23, 1921, and Milner to Jameson, Sept. 27, 1921, Jameson Papers.
11. Beckles Willson, *Friendly Relations*, p. 54.
12. Ibid., chap. 3, "The Tragi-Comedy of the Merrys," pp. 38–54.
13. Adams, *History of the United States,* vol. 2, chap. 16; "Anthony Merry," pp. 360–88; Irving Brant, *James Madison: Secretary of State, 1800–1809*, chap. 12, "Toujours Gai," pp. 160–76; Malone, *Jefferson the President: First Term*, chap. 20, "Without Benefit of Protocol: The Merry Affair," pp. 367–92.
14. Joel Larus, "Pell Mell along the Potomac"; Anthony Steel, "Anthony Merry and the Anglo-American Dispute about Impressment, 1803–1806."

Chapter I: Before the Mission to America

1. Parish Register of St. Laurence Pountney [also spelled St. Lawrence Poultney,], Baptisms, 1740–1812, MS 7667, Guildhall Library, London.
2. *London Directory*, 1780; John Franklin Jameson to Gerald H. Rendall, Oct. 5, 1921, John Franklin Jameson Papers, LC.
3. Sir William Burrell, *Reports of Cases Determined by the High Court of Admiralty*, pp. 1–2, 118–22.
4. Jameson to Rendall, Oct. 5, 1921, Jameson Papers.
5. *Gentleman's Magazine* (London) 52 (Apr. 1783):275; Anthony Merry to Charles James Fox, June 1, 1806, private, FO 5/49.
6. Robert Liston to the Marquis of Carmarthen, June 10, 1787, Osborne Papers, British Museum Additional MS 28062.

7. *Gentleman's Magazine* 57 (July 1787):646.

8. D. B. Horn, *The British Diplomatic Service, 1689–1789*, p. 51.

9. Codicil to the Will of Anthony Merry, Jan. 23, 1835, Probate Registry, Somerset House, London.

10. Rufus King to Secretary of State, Oct. 31, 1800, no. 88 in *Life and Correspondence of Rufus King*, 3:324–26.

11. This account of the Nootka Sound Affair is based on William R. Manning, "The Nootka Sound Controversy," and on John Holland Rose, *The Life of William Pitt*, 1:562–68.

12. Will of Anthony Merry, May 29, 1832, Probate Registry.

13. Lord St. Helens to Lord Grenville, June 15, 1791, Papers of Lord Grenville in Historical Manuscripts Commission, *Report on the Manuscripts of J. B. Fortescue, Esq., Preserved at Dropmore*, 2:99.

14. S. T. Bindoff, et al., *British Diplomatic Representatives, 1789–1852*, p. 140; Robert W. Seton-Watson, *Britain in Europe*, p. 372.

15. Bindoff et al., *British Diplomatic Representatives*, p. 41. *Gentleman's Magazine* 69 (June 1799):538.

16. Lord Brougham, Journal, Oct. 4, 1799, in *Life and Times of Henry, Lord Brougham*, 1:96, 99.

17. Bindoff et al., *British Diplomatic Representatives*, p. 48.

18. Quoted in Nicholas Biddle, "Private Journal."

19. Lord Glenbervie, Diary, Jan. 21, 1802, in *The Diaries of Sylvester Douglas, Lord Glenbervie*, 2:310.

20. Lord Malmesbury, Diary, Apr. 27 and May 2, 1802, in Malmesbury, *Diaries and Correspondence of James Harris, First Earl*, 4:73–76.

21. Lord Cornwallis to Alexander Ross, Feb. 13, 1802, in Cornwallis, *Correspondence*, 3:456–57.

22. Cornwallis to Lord Hawkesbury, Mar. 10 and Mar. 27, 1802, ibid., 3:468–69, 484.

23. Merry to Francis James Jackson, Feb. 25, 1802, FO 353/76.

24. Bindoff et al., *British Diplomatic Representatives*, pp. 48, 140; Hawkesbury to the king, Mar. 31, 1802, in *Later Correspondence of George III*, 4:21–22; Merry to Arthur Paget, Apr. 26, 1802, in Paget, *Diplomatic and Other Correspondence*, 2:56.

25. Charles Duke Yonge, *The Life and Administration of Robert Banks, Second Earl of Liverpool, K. G. . . . ,* 1:91–93.

26. Merry to Jackson, July 18 and Sept. 20, 1802, FO 353/76; Fanny Burney (Madame d'Arblay), Paris Journal, Apr. 24–25, 1802, in *The Journals and Letters of Fanny Burney*, 5:270; Fanny Burney to Miss Planta, Apr. 27, 1802, ibid., 5:293; prefatory notes to letters, ibid., 5:278, 288, 321, 332, 334, 336, 353, 362, 374.

27. John B. Alger, *Napoleon's British Visitors and Captives, 1801–1815*, pp. 21–22, 31; Lady Bessborough to Lord Granville, Oct. [?], 1802, in Earl Granville, *Private Correspondence, 1781–1821*, 1:366.

28. Quoted in John Campbell, Baron, *Lives of the Lord Chancellors and Keepers of the Great Seal of England,* 8:362–63.

29. Merry to Jackson, July 18 and Sept. 20, 1802, FO 353/76.

30. Alger, *Napoleon's British Visitors and Captives*, p. 128.

31. Rendall to Jameson, Aug. 28, 1921, Jameson Papers; Gerald H. Rendall, *Dedham Described and Deciphered*, p. 59; *The Port Folio* (Philadelphia) 4 (Feb. 11, 1804): 1947. Merry's seal with the motto "toujours gai" was seen by Jameson in London in 1921, when it was in the possession of a collateral descendant. Jameson to Rendall, Oct. 5, 1921, Jameson Papers.

32. Jameson, "The Approach to Diplomatic History by the Correspondence of the Early British Ministers to the United States," unpublished lecture, Jameson Papers.

33. William Johnston Temple, Diary, July 8 and Sept. 28, 1795, in *Diaries of William Johnston Temple*, pp. 128, 144; Manasseh Cutler to Mrs. Poole, Feb. 28, 1804, and to Mrs. Torrey, Feb. 21, 1805, in Cutler, *Life, Journals, and Correspondence*, 2:163–64, 189–91.

34. Reproduced in this book on p. 11 from plate in Lawrence Park, *Gilbert Stuart*, 4:330; see also notes 2:523.

35. Augustus John Foster to Lady Elizabeth Foster, July 20, 1806, Augustus John Foster Papers, LC; Thomas Moore to his mother, Sept. [?], 1803, in Thomas Moore, *Memoirs, Journal, and Correspondence*, 1:134.

36. Merry to Jackson, Sept. 20, 1803, FO 353/76; Temple, *Diaries*, p. 123.

37. Will of Anthony Merry, May 29, 1832, Probate Registry.

38. Merry to Jackson, July 18, 1802, FO 353/76.

39. Merry to Jackson, Sept. 20, 1802, FO 353/76.

40. *Gentleman's Magazine* 73 (Jan. 1803):83.

Chapter II: Minister to the United States

1. *Gentleman's Magazine* (London) 73 (Apr. 1803):375.

2. Rufus King to secretary of state, Sept. 30, 1800, no. 84 in *Life and Correspondence of Rufus King*, 3:313–15.

3. King to secretary of state, Oct. 31, 1800, no. 88, ibid., 3:324–26.

4. King to secretary of state, Apr. 10, 1802, no. 62, ibid.., 4:100–101.

5. Lord Malmesbury, Diary, Feb. 16, 1803, in Malmesbury, *Diaries and Correspondence of James Harris, First Earl*, 4:208.

6. King to secretary of state, Apr. 30, 1802, No. 63 in King, *Life and Correspondence*, 4:112–13.

7. Anthony Merry to Francis James Jackson, Sept. 20, 1802, FO 353/76.

8. Merry to Jackson, Oct. 8, 1802, FO 353/76.

9. King to secretary of state, Mar. 17, 1803, no. 85 in King, *Life and Correspondence*, 4:229–30.

10. John W. Osborne, *William Cobbett*, p. 22.

11. *Cobbett's Annual Register* (London) 3 (Apr. 9–16, 1803):571–72.

12. Ibid., 3 (Apr. 23–30, 1803):628–29.

13. Merry to King, Feb. 26, 1803, Rufus King Papers, New-York Historical Society, New York.

14. King, Memorandum, May 8, 1803, in King, *Life and Correspondence*, 4:253–54.

15. James Monroe to James Madison, Sept. 18, 1803, William Cabell Rives Papers, LC.

16. Christopher Gore to King, Sept. 30, 1803, In King, *Life and Correspondence*, 4:309–11; Edward Thornton to Lord Hawkesbury, Dec. 6, 1803, no. 54, FO 5/38.

17. Merry to Madison, Nov. 4, 1803, Notes from the British Legation, vol. 3, SDR.

18. Thomas Moore to his mother, Nov. 7, 1803, in Thomas Moore, *Memoirs, Journal and Correspondence*, 1:137–42.

19. Thornton to Hawkesbury, Dec. 6, 1803, no. 54, FO 5/38; Merry to Hawkesbury, Dec. 6, 1803, no. 1, FO 5/41.

20. Elizabeth Merry to Moore, n.d. [after Nov. 26, 1803], in Moore, *Memoirs*, 8:50–52.

21. Ibid.

22. Merry to Madison, Nov. 26, 1803, Notes from the British Legation, vol. 3, SDR.

23. Merry to Madison, May 4, 1804, ibid.

24. King to Gore, Dec. 7, 1803, in King, *Life and Correspondence*, 4:327.

25. Merry to George Hammond, Dec. 7, 1803, private, FO 5/41. The two "mere shells" of houses stood on the south side of K Street in Washington between Twenty-sixth and Twenty-seventh streets, NW, and in later years were numbered 2618 and 2620. This first British legation in Washington (see picture, p. 32) was also the first foreign legation established in the new capital. House number 2618 was historic for another reason: George Washington's stepgranddaughter lived there before the Merrys, and Washington slept in that house on his last visit to the capital city. On another occasion John Adams also stayed in the house. The two houses were demolished in 1961 to make way for a highway interchange. (Harold Donaldson Eberlain and Cortlandt Van Dyke Hubbard, *Historic Houses of George-Town & Washington City*, pp. 342–43).

26. Hawkesbury to Thornton, Sept. 16, 1803, no. 2 in Bernard Mayo, ed., *Instructions to the British Ministers to the United States, 1791–1812*, p. 96; Merry to Hawkesbury, July 13, 1804, separate, FO 5/42.

27. Elizabeth Merry to Thomas Moore, n.d. [after Nov. 26, 1803], in Moore, *Memoirs*, 8:50–52.

28. Thornton to Hawkesbury, Mar. 1, 1803, separate, FO 5/38.

29. Alexander Baring to Robert Liston, Sept. 22, 1802, Sir Robert Liston Papers, National Library of Scotland, Edinburgh.

30. Henry Adams, *History of the United States during the Administrations of Thomas Jefferson and James Madison*, 2:361.

31. Augustus John Foster to Lady Elizabeth Foster, Mar. 27 and Nov. 27, 1806, Augustus John Foster Papers, LC.

32. Foster to Lady Elizabeth Foster, Sept. 2, 1805, and July 20, 1806, ibid.

33. Stanley Lane-Pool, *Life of the Right Hon. Stratford Canning, Viscount Stratford de Redcliffe*, 1:30.

34. William Plumer, Memorandum, Mar. 11, 1806, in Plumer, *Memorandum of Proceedings in the United States Senate, 1803–1807*, pp. 447–48.

35. George Jackson, Diaries, Jan. 23, 1812, in Jackson, *The Bath Archives*, 1:317–21; Madison to Monroe, July 21, 1804, private, James Monroe Papers, LC.

36. Thomas Jefferson to James Maury, Apr. 25, 1812, in Jefferson, *The Writings of Thomas Jefferson* (Ford ed.), 9:348–51.

37. Benjamin Ogle Tayloe to [?], Dec. 15, 1866, in Winslow Marston Watson, *In Memoriam: Benjamin Ogle Tayloe*, pp. 239–40.

38. Foster to Lady Elizabeth Foster, Dec. 30, 1804, Foster Papers.

39. Merry to Hammond, Oct. 1, 1804, private, FO 5/42.

40. Foster to Lady Elizabeth Foster, Aug. 30, 1806, Foster Papers.

41. Madison to Monroe, Dec. 26, 1803, in Madison, *The Writings of James Madison*, 6:76–78; Madison to Monroe, July 21, 1804, Monroe Papers.

42. Jefferson to Monroe, Jan. 8, 1804, in Jefferson, *Writings* (Ford ed.), 4:286–92.

43. Manasseh Cutler to Mrs. Poole, Feb. 28, 1804, in Cutler, *Life, Journals, and Correspondence*, 2:163–64.

44. Margaret Bayard Smith to Mrs. Kirkpatrick, Jan. 23, 1804, in Smith, *The First Forty Years of Washington Society*, pp. 44–47.

45. Jefferson to Monroe, Jan. 8, 1804, in Jefferson, *Writings* (Ford ed.), 4:286–92.

46. Margaret Bayard Smith to Mrs. Kirkpatrick, Jan. 23, 1804, in Smith, *The First Forty Years*, pp. 44–47.

47. Aaron Burr to Theodosia, Jan. 17, 1804, in *Memoirs of Aaron Burr with Miscellaneous Selections from His Correspondence*, 2:269.

48. Cutler to Mrs. Poole, Feb. 28, 1804, and to Mrs. Torrey, Feb. 21, 1805, in Cutler, *Life*, 2:163–64, 189–91; Cutler to Jonathan Stokes, May 15, 1805, in Allen Culling Clark, *Life and Letters of Dolly Madison*, p. 77.

49. Elizabeth Merry to Cutler, May 17, 1806, in Cutler, *Life*, 2:280–81; Cutler, Journal, June 26, 1806, ibid., 2:335.

50. Cutler to Mrs. Torrey, Feb. 21, 1805, ibid., 2:189–91.

51. Foster to Lady Elizabeth Foster, June 2, 1805, and July 20, 1806, Foster Papers.

52. Thomas Moore to his mother, June 13, 1804, in Moore, *Memoirs*, 1:161–63.

53. George Jackson, Diary and Letters, Jan. 23, 1812, in Jackson, *The Bath Archives*, 1:317–21.

54. Elizabeth Merry to Moore, n.d. [after Nov. 26, 1803], in Moore, *Memoirs*, 8:50–52.

55. Ibid.

56. *Aurora* (Philadelphia), Nov. 25, 1803, enclosure in Merry to Hawkesbury, Dec. 6, 1803, no. 5, FO 5/41.

57. Thornton to Hawkesbury, Jan. 31, 1803, no. 8, FO 5/38.

58. Jefferson to Sir John Sinclair, June 30, 1803 in *The Writings of Thomas Jefferson* (Lipscomb and Bergh ed.), 10:396–98.

59. Jefferson to Robert R. Livingston, Apr. 18, 1802, ibid., 10:311–16.

60. Madison to Thornton, July 22, 1803, enclosure in Thornton to Hawkesbury, July 29, 1803, no. 36, FO 5/38.

61. Madison to Thornton, Aug. 5, 1803, enclosure in Thornton to Hawkesbury, Aug. 26, 1803, no. 41, FO 5/38.

62. Thornton to Hawkesbury, Aug. 26, 1803, no. 41, FO 5/38.

63. Hawkesbury to Merry, Sept. 16, 1803, nos. 1, 2, 3, 4 in Mayo, ed., *Instructions to the British Ministers*, pp. 197–201.

64. Monroe to Madison, Sept. 29, 1803, no. 15, Despatches from the United States Ministers to Great Britain, vol. 12, SDR.

65. Gore to King, Sept. 30, 1803, in King, *Life and Correspondence*, 4:309–11.

66. Thornton to Hawkesbury, Oct. 3, 1803, no. 46, FO 5/38.

67. Thornton to Hawkesbury, Oct. 28, 1803, no. 50, FO 5/38.

68. Thornton to Hawkesbury, Oct. 31, 1803, separate, FO 5/38.

69. Thornton to Hawkesbury, Nov. 1, 1803, no. 52, FO 5/38.

70. Thornton to Hammond, Jan. 29, 1804, private, FO 5/41.

Chapter III: "A Foolish Circumstance of Etiquette"

1. Dumas Malone, *Jefferson the President: First Term, 1801–1805,* p. 389.

2. Beckles Willson, *Friendly Relations,* p. 38.

3. Anthony Merry to Lord Hawkesbury, Dec. 6, 1803, separate, FO 5/41.

4. Thomas Jefferson to William Short, Jan. 23, 1804, in *American Historical Review* 33 (1928):833.

5. Augustus John Foster to Lady Elizabeth Foster, Dec. 30, 1804, Augustus John Foster Papers, LC.

6. Merry to Hawkesbury, Dec. 6, 1804, no. 1, FO 5/41; Josiah Quincy, Journal, Jan. 1806, in Edmund Quincy, *Life of Josiah Quincy*, pp. 92–93.

7. Samuel Taggart to John Taylor, Jan. 13, 1804, in "Letters of Samuel Taggart, Representative in Congress, 1803–1814," pp. 120–25.

8. Quoted in Josiah Quincy, Journal, Jan. 1806, in Quincy, *Life of Josiah Quincy*, pp. 92–93.

9. Stanley Lane-Pool, *Life of the Right Hon. Stratford Canning, Viscount Stratford de Redcliffe*, 1:315–16.

10. Merry to Hawkesbury, Dec. 6, 1803, private, FO 5/41.

11. Jefferson to James Monroe, Jan. 8, 1804, in Jefferson, *The Writings of Thomas Jefferson* (Ford ed.), 8:286; James Madison to Monroe, Feb. 16, 1804, in Madison, *The Writings of James Madison*, 7:118–21.

12. Merry to Hawkesbury, Dec. 31, 1803, separate, FO 5/41.

13. Louis André Pichon to Talleyrand, Feb. 5, 1804, in Affaires Etrangerès,

Correspondence Politique, Etats-Unis (transcripts in Library of Congress from French Archives).

14. Allen Culling Clark, *Life and Letters of Dolly Madison*, p. 61.

15. Sir Augustus John Foster, *Jeffersonian America*, p. 52.

16. Clark, *Life and Letters of Dolly Madison*, p. 62.

17. Merry to Hawkesbury, Dec. 6, 1803, separate, FO 5/41.

18. Foster, *Jeffersonian America*, p. 21.

19. Ibid., p. 52.

20. Merry to Hawkesbury, Dec. 6, 1803, separate, FO 5/41.

21. Merry to George Hammond, Dec. 7, 1803, private FO 5/41.

22. Jefferson to Short, Jan. 23, 1804, in *American Historical Review* 33 (1928):833.

23. Pichon to Talleyrand, Feb. 5, 1804, Affaires Etrangères.

24. Clark, *Life and Letters of Dolly Madison*, pp. 64–65.

25. Merry to Hammond, Dec. 7, 1803, private, FO 5/41.

26. Madison to Rufus King, Dec. 18, 1803, in King, *Life and Correspondence of Rufus King*, 4:332–33.

27. King to Madison, Dec. 22, 1803, Thomas Jefferson Papers, LC.

28. Timothy Pickering to Richard Peters, Dec. 24, 1803, Timothy Pickering Papers, Massachusetts Historical Society, Boston.

29. Foster, *Jeffersonian America*, pp. 52–55.

30. Pichon to Talleyrand, Feb. 5, 1804, Affaires Etrangères; Irving Brant, *James Madison: Secretary of State, 1800–1809*, p. 164.

31. Elizabeth Merry to Jefferson, Dec. 26, 1803, Thomas Jefferson Papers, Massachusetts Historical Society.

32. Jefferson to Monroe, Jan. 28, 1804, in Jefferson, *Writings* (Ford ed.), 4:286–92.

33. Merry to Hawkesbury, Dec. 31, 1803, separate, FO 5/41.

34. Pichon to Talleyrand, Feb. 5, 1804, Affaires Etrangères.

35. Malone, *Jefferson the President: First Term*, pp. 383–84; Margaret Bayard Smith to Mrs. Kirkpatrick, Jan. 23, 1804, in Smith, *The First Forty Years of Washington Society*, pp. 44–47.

36. Merry to Hammond, Dec. 7, 1803, private, FO 5/41.

37. Pichon to Talleyrand, Feb. 5, 1804, Affaires Etrangères.

38. King to Christopher Gore, Jan. 4, 1804, in King, *Life and Correspondence*, 4:340.

39. Madison to Monroe, Dec. 26, 1803, private, in Madison, *Writings*, 7:76.

40. Rules of Etiquette, n.d. [before Jan. 12, 1804], in Jefferson, *Writings* (Ford ed.), 8:276–77.

41. Madison to Monroe, Jan. 19, 1804, William Cabell Rives Papers, LC; Merry to Hawkesbury, Jan. 30, 1804, separate, FO 5/41; Madison to Monroe, Feb. 16, 1804, in Madison, *Writings* 8:118–21.

42. Pichon to Talleyrand, Feb. 5, 1804, Affaires Etrangères.

43. Margaret Bayard Smith to Mrs. Kirkpatrick, Jan. 23, 1804, in Smith, *The First Forty Years*, 46.

44. Ibid., 404–5.

45. *Gazette of the United States* (Philadelphia), Jan. 17, 1804 (country edition).

46. Malone, *Jefferson the President: First Term*, p. 387.

47. *Aurora* (Philadelphia), Feb. 13, 1804.

48. Nathaniel Macon to John Steele, Feb. 12, 1804, in Kemp P. Battle, ed., *"Letters of Nathaniel Macon, John Steele, and William Barry Grove,"* pp. 48–50.

49. Foster, *Jeffersonian America*, p. 53.

50. Merry to Madison, Feb. 9, 1804, in Madison, *Writings*, 7:121–23.

51. Pichon to Talleyrand, Feb. 13, 1804, Affaires Etrangères.

52. Madison to Monroe, Dec. 26, 1803, in Madison, *Writings*, 7:76–78.

53. Jefferson to Monroe, Jan. 8, 1804, in Jefferson, *Writings* (Ford ed.), 4:286–92.

54. Foster, *Jeffersonian America*, pp. 54–55.

55. Edward Thornton to Hawkesbury, Mar. 11, 1803, separate, FO 5/38.

56. Merry to Hawkesbury, Jan. 30, 1804, separate, FO 5/41; Francis James Jackson to George Jackson, Oct. 20, 1809, in Sir George Jackson, *The Bath Archives*, 1:22–29.

57. Gore to King, Feb. 8, 1804, in King, *Life and Correspondence*, 4:341–43.

58. Monroe to Madison, Mar. 3, 1804, in Monroe, *The Writings of James Monroe*, 4:148–52.

59. *Cobbett's Weekly Political Register* (London) 5 (Feb. 18, 1804):250–51.

60. Monroe to Madison, Mar. 3, 1804, in Monroe, *Writings*, 4:148–152.

61. Monroe to Madison, Apr. 26, 1804, ibid., 4:170–71.

62. Gore to King, Apr. 17, 1804, in King, *Life and Correspondence*, 4:386–87.

63. Monroe to Madison, Apr. 26, 1804, in Monroe, *Writings*, 4:170–174.

64. Monroe to Madison, July 1, 1804, ibid., 4:218–23.

65. Monroe to Madison, June 28, 1804, ibid., 208–10.

66. Monroe to Madison, July 1, 1804, ibid., 4:218–23.

67. George Jackson to [?], July 2, 1804, in Jackson, *Diaries and Letters of Sir George Jackson*, 1:212–14.

68. Francis James Jackson to George Jackson, Oct. 20, 1809, in Sir George Jackson, *The Bath Archives*, 1:22–29.

69. Henry Suttle to Merry, May 10, 1804, and Madison to Merry, May 19 and 22, 1804, enclosures in Merry to Hawkesbury, June 1, 1804, separate, FO 5/41.

70. Merry to Madison, May 4, 1804, Notes from the British Legation, vol. 3, SDR; Merry to Hawkesbury, June 1, 1804, separate, FO 5/41.

71. Harold Donaldson Eberlain and Cortlandt Van Dyke Hubbard, *Historic Houses of George-Town & Washington City*, p. 194.

72. Madison to Monroe, July 21, 1804, private, James Monroe Papers, LC.

73. Foster, *Jeffersonian America*, pp. 10–11; Howard Mumford Jones, *The Harp That Once—*, pp. 77–78.

74. Jacob Wagner to Madison, Sept. 1 and 15, 1804, James Madison Papers, LC; Malone, *Jefferson the President: First Term*, p. 391.

75. Madison to Jefferson, Aug. 28, 1804, Jefferson Papers, LC.

76. Merry to Madison, Sept. 14, 1805, Notes from the British Legation, vol. 3, SDR.

77. Foster to Lady Elizabeth Foster, Dec. 30, 1804, Foster Papers.

78. Foster, *Jeffersonian America*, pp. 22–23.

79. Merry to Lord Mulgrave, Mar. 2, 1806, no. 10, FO 5/48; Foster, *Jeffersonian America*, p. 50; *Annals of Congress*, 9th Cong., 1st sess. (1805–6), pp. 92–94, 166.

80. Foster to Lady Elizabeth Foster, July 20, 1806, Foster Papers. Manasseh Cutler to Mrs. Poole, Feb. 21, 1804, in Cutler, *Life, Journals, and Correspondence*, 2:163.

81. Foster, *Jeffersonian America*, p. 53, editor's n. 65.

82. Henry Adams, *History of the United States during the Administrations of Thomas Jefferson and James Madison*, 2:390.

Chapter IV: Defender of a Vital British Interest

1. James Fulton Zimmerman, *Impressment of American Seamen*, pp. 260–61.

2. Anthony Merry to Lord Hawkesbury, Dec. 6, 1803, nos. 1 and 2, FO 5/41.

3. Merry to Hawkesbury, Dec. 31, 1803, no. 6, FO 5/41.

4. James Madison to James Monroe, Jan. 5, 1804, in Madison, *The Writings of James Madison*, 7:79–80.

5. Merry to Hawkesbury, Jan. 20, 1804, no. 12, FO 5/41.

6. Merry to Hawkesbury, Jan. 30, 1804, no. 13, FO 5/41.

7. Merry to Hawkesbury, Mar. 4, 1804, no. 21, FO 5/41.

8. Edward Thornton to George Hammond, Jan. 29, 1804, private, FO 5/41.

9. Thomas Barclay to Adm. Sir Andrew Mitchell, Nov. 21, 1803, in Barclay, *Selections from the Correspondence of Thomas Barclay*, p. 154.

10. Merry to Hawkesbury, Apr. 29, 1804, no. 30, FO 5/41.

11. Merry to Hawkesbury, June 2, 1804, no. 34, FO 5/41.

12. Barclay to Hammond, June 27, 1804, FO 5/43.

13. DeWitt Clinton to Barclay, June 17, 1804, enclosure in Merry to Hawkesbury, July 2, 1804, no. 36, FO 5/42.

14. Barclay to Clinton, June 18, 1804, in Barclay, *Correspondence*, pp. 163–64.

15. Order of New York Mayor to Pilots, June 18, 1804, enclosure in Merry to Hawkesbury, July 2, 1804, no. 36, FO 5/42.

16. Clinton to Barclay, June 18, 1804, FO 5/43.

17. Barclay to Capt. William Bradley, June 19, 1804, in Barclay, *Correspondence*, pp. 165–66.

18. Merry to Hawkesbury, July 2, 1804, no. 36, FO 5/42.

19. Barclay to Merry, June 30, 1804, in Barclay, *Correspondence*, pp. 172–74.

20. Madison to Merry, July 3, 1804, enclosure in Merry to Hawkesbury, July 18, 1804, no. 40, FO 5/42.

21. Madison to Merry, July 7, 1804, enclosure in Merry to Hawkesbury, July 18, 1804, no. 40, FO 5/42.

22. Merry to Lord Harrowby, July 18, 1804, no. 40, FO 5/42.

23. Barclay to Merry, Aug. 14, 1804, in Barclay, *Correspondence*, pp. 184–85.

24. Merry to Madison, Aug. 15, 1804, enclosure in Merry to Harrowby, Sept. 4, 1804, no. 45, FO 5/42; Capt. Bradley to Adm. Sir Andrew Mitchell, July 14, 1804, Adm. 1/495.

25. Madison to Thomas Jefferson, Aug. 28, 1804, Thomas Jefferson Papers, LC.

26. Phineas Bond to Hammond, June 30, 1804, FO 5/43.

27. John Barrow to Adm. Mitchell, Aug. 16, 1804, Adm. 2/931; Barrow to Hammond, Aug. 16, 1804, FO 5/44.

28. Barclay to Merry, Aug. 24, 1804, in Barclay, *Correspondence*, pp. 188–90.

29. Merry to Capt. Bradley, Aug. 25, 1804, Adm. 1/1582.

30. Madison to Merry, Sept. 3, 1804, enclosure in Merry to Harrowby, Oct. 1, 1804, no. 51, FO 5/42.

31. Merry to Harrowby, Sept. 4, 1804, no. 45, Fo 5/45.

32. Harrowby to Merry, Nov. 7, 1804, no. 3 in Bernard Mayo, ed., *Instructions to the British Ministers to the United States, 1791–1812*, pp. 208–11.

33. Merry to Harrowby, Feb. 14, 1805, no. 4, FO 5/45.

34. Merry to Lord Mulgrave, June 30, 1805, no. 26, FO 5/45.

35. Madison to Merry, Mar. 28, 1805, enclosure in Merry to Harrowby, Mar. 30, 1805, no. 17, FO 5/45.

36. Merry to Mulgrave, Apr. 29, 1805, no. 20, FO 5/45.

37. Madison to Merry, Apr. 9, 1805, enclosure, ibid.

38. Merry to Madison, Apr. 12, 1805, Notes from the British Legation, vol. 3, SDR.

39. Barclay to Merry, Apr. 16, 1805, in Barclay, *Correspondence*, pp. 218–20.

40. Jefferson, Special Message to Congress, Jan. 17, 1806, in James D. Richardson, ed., *A Compilation of the Messages and Papers of the Presidents, 1789–1908*, 1:395.

41. Merry to Mulgrave, Feb. 2, 1806, no. 7, FO 5/48.

42. Merry to Madison, Aug. 18, 1806, Notes from the British Legation, vol. 3, SDR.

43. Merry to Charles James Fox, Aug. 31, 1806, n. 41, FO 5/49.

44. Merry to Fox, Nov. 2, 1806, no. 50, FO 5/49.

45. Merry to Harrowby, Dec. 4, 1804, no. 63, FO 5/42.

46. *United States Statutes at Large*, vol. 2, pp. 339–42.

47. Merry to Harrowby, Mar. 4, 1805, no. 9, FO 5/45.

48. Ibid.

49. Merry to Mulgrave, June 30, 1805, no. 26, FO 5/45.

50. Jefferson, Message to Congress, Dec. 3, 1805, in Richardson, ed., *Messages and Papers*, 1:383.

51. Merry to Harrowby, Mar. 4, 1805, no. 8, FO 5/48, with enclosures of Merry to Madison, Feb. 23, 1805, and Madison to Merry, Feb. 26, 1805.

52. Merry to Madison, Jan. 6, 1806, enclosure in Merry to Fox, May 3, 1806, no. 21, FO 5/49.

53. Madison to Merry, Jan. 7, 1806, ibid.

54. Merry to Madison, Apr. 14, 1806, ibid.

55. Merry to Fox, May 3, 1806, no. 21, FO 5/49.

56. Merry to Fox, May 4, 1806, no. 24, FO 5/49; Merry to Barclay, May 3, 1806, Adm. 1/496.

57. Merry to Madison, May 9, 1806, enclosure in Merry to Fox, May 9, 1806, no. 25, FO 5/49.

58. Jefferson to Jacob Crowninshield, May 13, 1806, in Jefferson, *The Writings of Thomas Jefferson* (Ford ed.), 8:451–53.

59. Merry to Fox, June 1, 1806, no. 26, FO 5/49.

60. Fox to Merry, June 6, 1806, no. 5, in Mayo, ed., *Instructions to the British Ministers*, p. 223.

61. Merry to Fox, Aug. 3, 1806, no. 35, FO 5/49.

62. Merry to Fox, Sept. 28, 1806, no. 47, FO 5/49; Merry to Fox, Nov. 2, 1806, no. 33, FO 5/49; David M. Erskine to Lord Howick, Mar. 1, 1807, no. 6, FO 5/52.

63. Madison to Merry, Dec. 24, 1803, enclosure in Merry to Hawkesbury, Dec. 31, 1803, no. 6, FO 5/41.

64. Madison to Thornton, Oct. 27, 1803, in Carlton Savage, ed., *Policy of the United States toward Maritime Commerce in War*, 1:241–42.

65. Evan Nepean to Hammond, Jan. 5, 1804, vol. 3 (1832) in *American State Papers: Foreign Relations*, pp. 265–66.

66. Merry to Hawkesbury, April 29, 1804, no. 30, FO 5/41.

67. Merry to Madison, Aug. 31, 1804, enclosure in Merry to Hawkesbury, Sept. 4, 1804, no. 46, FO 5/42.

68. Merry to Mulgrave, Jan. 25, 1805, no. 2, FO 5/45.

69. Mulgrave to Merry, Mar. 8, 1805, no. 1 in Mayo, ed., *Instructions to the British Ministers*, pp. 214–15.

70. Merry to Hawkesbury, Apr. 10, 1804, no. 27, FO 5/41.

71. Merry to Mulgrave, Jan. 31, 1806, no. 5, FO 5/48.

72. Merry to Fox, June 29, 1806, no. 34, FO 5/49.

73. Merry to Fox, Aug. 3, 1806, no. 39, FO 5/49.

74. Fox to Merry, Apr. 8, 1806, no. 4 in Mayo, ed., *Instructions to the British Minister*, p. 222.

75. Fox to Merry, May 16, 1806, circular, ibid.

76. Merry to Fox, June 1, 1806, no. 29, FO 5/49.

77. Merry to Fox, June 29, 1806, no. 33, FO 5/49.

78. Merry to Mulgrave, Sept. 30, 1805, no. 40, FO 5/45.

79. Merry to Mulgrave, Nov. 3, 1805, no. 44, FO 5/45.

80. Henry Adams, *History of the United States during the Administrations of Thomas Jefferson and James Madison*, 1:63.

81. Merry to Mulgrave, Nov. 3, 1805, no. 44, FO 5/45. Adams, *History of the United States*, vol. 2, chaps. 2 and 3 passim; Issac J. Cox, *The West Florida Controversy, 1798–1818*, pp. 34, 75, 146–47, 182–83.

82. Merry to Mulgrave, Nov. 3, 1805, no. 45, FO 5/45.

83. John Armstrong to Madison, Sept. 10, 1805, Despatches from the United States Ministers to France, vol. 10, SDR.

84. Merry to Mulgrave, Dec. 2, 1805, no. 50, FO 5/45.

85. Merry to Mulgrave, Dec. 3, 1805, no. 52, FO 5/45; Jefferson, Fifth Annual Message to Congress, Dec. 3, 1805, in Richardson, ed., *Messages and Papers*, 1:384.

86. Merry to Mulgrave, Jan. 3, 1806, no. 1, FO 5/48.

87. Merry to Adm. Mitchell, Jan. 14, 1806, Adm. 1/496.

88. Merry to Mulgrave, Feb. 2, 1806, no. 7, FO 5/48.

89. Merry to Mulgrave, Feb. 24, 1806, no. 9, FO 5/48.

90. Merry to Mulgrave, Mar. 6, 1806, no. 13, FO 5/48.

91. Merry to Mulgrave, Mar. 2, 1806, no. 10, FO 5/48.

92. Merry to Fox, Apr. 20, 1806, no. 20, FO 5/48.

93. Merry to Mulgrave, Mar. 2, 1806, no. 10, FO 5/48.

94. Merry to Fox, May 4, 1806, no. 23, FO 5/49.

95. Ibid.

Chapter V: Observer and Reporter

1. Edward Thornton to Lord Hawkesbury, Mar. 11, 1803, separate, FO 5/38.

2. Augustus John Foster to Lady Elizabeth Foster, July 20, 1806, Augustus John Foster Papers, LC.

3. Manasseh Cutler, Journal, Feb. 12 and 26, 1805, in Cutler, *Life, Journals, and Correspondence*, 2:183.

4. Sir Augustus John Foster, *Jeffersonian America*, p. 52.

5. William Plumer, Memorandum, Dec. 1, 1805, in Plumer, *Memorandum of Proceedings in the United States Senate, 1803–1807*, p. 338.

6. Ralph Ketcham, *James Madison*, p. 478.

7. Anthony Merry to George Hammond, Mar. 4, 1804, private, FO 5/41; Merry to Hawkesbury, June 3, 1804, no. 35, FO 5/42.

8. Thomas Barclay to Merry, July 13, 1804, in Barclay, *Selections from the Correspondence of Thomas Barclay*, p. 177.

9. Phineas Bond to Hammond, Aug. 6, 1804, FO 5/43.

10. Barclay to Adm. Sir Andrew Mitchell, Aug. 25, 1804, in Barclay, *Correspondence*, pp. 190–92.

11. Merry to Hammond, Oct. 1, 1804, private, FO 5/42; Thomas William Moore to Stratford Canning, Sept. 30, 1822, FO 352/8.

12. Merry to Hammond, Nov. 21, 1804, private, FO 5/42; Merry to Lord Harrowby, Dec. 26, 1804, no. 64, FO 5/42.

13. Foster to Lady Elizabeth Foster, Dec. 30, 1804, Foster Papers.

14. Foster to Lady Elizabeth Foster, June 2, 1805, Foster Papers.

15. Merry to James Madison, Sept. 14, 1805, Notes from the British Legation, vol. 3, SDR; Merry to Lord Mulgrave, Sept. 30, 1805, no. 4, FO 5/43.

16. Foster to Lady Elizabeth Foster, Sept. 2 and 22, Nov. 7, 1805, Foster Papers.

17. Merry to Charles James Fox, Sept. 28, 1806, no. 45, FO 5/49; Foster, *Jeffersonian America*, pp. 222, 243.

18. Francis James Jackson to Mrs. Jackson, Oct. 7, 1809, in Sir George Jackson, *The Bath Archives*, 1:17–22.

19. Foster, *Jeffersonian America*, p. 211.

20. Ibid., pp. 115–17.

21. Adm. Mitchell to Merry, Jan. 25, 1804, Adm. 1/495.

22. Merry to Adm. Mitchell, Feb. 3, 1804, Adm. 1/495.

23. Adm. Mitchell to William Marsden, Apr. 1, 1804, Adm. 1/495.

24. Merry to Hawkesbury, Mar. 4, 1804, no. 22, and Mar. 31, 1804, no. 26, FO 5/41; John Hamilton to Adm. Mitchell, Apr. 9, 1804, Adm. 1/495; Merry to Fox, Sept. 6, 1806, no. 43, FO 5/49.

25. Merry to Harrowby, June 3, 1804, no. 35, Sept. 4, 1804, no. 47, and Dec. 27, 1804, no. 65, FO 5/42; Merry to Harrowby, Jan. 2, 1805, no. 1, FO 5/45.

26. Merry to Hawkesbury, Apr. 15, 1804, no. 28, FO 5/41.

27. Lord Mulgrave to Merry, June 5, 1805, no. 6 in Bernard Mayo, ed., *Instructions to the British Ministers to the United States, 1791–1812*, p. 217; Merry to Mulgrave, Sept. 30, 1805, no. 39, FO 5/45.

28. Merry to Fox, Aug. 3, 1806, no. 39, FO 5/49.

29. Merry to Hawkesbury, Dec. 6, 1803, no. 4, FO 5/41.

30. Merry to Harrowby, Mar. 29, 1805, no. 13, FO 5/45; Merry to Fox, May 4, 1806, no. 23, FO 5/49.

31. Merry to Fox, Nov. 2, 1806, no. 51, FO 5/49.

32. Merry to Hawkesbury, Dec. 6, 1803, no. 5, FO 5/41; Marshall Smelser, *The Democratic Republic, 1801–1815*, p. 74.

33. Merry to Hawkesbury, Mar. 4, 1804, no. 22, FO 5/41.

34. Merry to Hawkesbury, Mar. 31, 1804, no. 25, FO 5/41.

35. Merry to Hawkesbury, Apr. 29, 1804, no. 30, FO 5/41; Merry to Hawkesbury, May 7, 1804, no. 32, FO 5/41.

36. Merry to Hawkesbury, June 2, 1804, no. 33, FO 5/42.

37. Merry to Hawkesbury, July 2, 1804, no. 37, FO 5/42; Merry to Hawkesbury, July 18, 1804, no. 41, FO 5/42.

38. Merry to Hammond, Oct. 1, 1804, private, FO 5/42.

39. Merry to Harrowby, Jan. 25, 1805, no. 2, FO 5/45.

40. Merry to Harrowby, Mar. 29, 1805, no. 14, FO 5/45.

41. Merry to Mulgrave, Apr. 29, 1805, no. 21, FO 5/45.

42. Merry to Mulgrave, Feb. 1, 1806, no. 6, FO 5/48.

43. Harry Ammon, *James Monroe*, p. 254.

44. Merry to Fox, May 4, 1806, no. 22, FO 5/49.

45. Merry to Fox, May 4, 1806, no. 23, FO 5/49.

46. Merry to Fox, Aug. 31, 1806, no. 42, FO 5/49.

47. Sir Francis Vincent to Merry, Aug. 8, 1806, separate, in Mayo, ed., *Instructions to the British Ministers*, p. 224; Merry to Fox, Nov. 2, 1806, no. 49, FO 5/49; Smelser, *The Democratic Republic*, p. 167.

48. Merry to Hawkesbury, Mar. 4, 1804, no. 20, FO 5/41.

49. Merry to Hawkesbury, Mar. 13, 1804, no. 23, FO 5/41.

50. Ibid.

51. Merry to Hawkesbury, Mar. 31, 1804, no. 25, FO 5/41.

52. Merry to Hawkesbury, Apr. 15, 1804, no. 28, FO 5/41.

53. Thomas Perkins Abernethy, *The South in the New Nation: 1789-1819*, p. 264.

54. Merry to Harrowby, Sept. 4, 1804, no. 47, FO 5/42.

55. Merry to Harrowby, Mar. 29, 1805, no. 14, FO 5/45.

56. W. Stull Holt, *Treaties Defeated by the Senate*, pp. 19-24.

57. Merry to Hawkesbury, Dec. 6, 1803, no. 3, FO 5/41.

58. Merry to Hawkesbury, Jan. 30, 1804, no. 14, FO 5/41.

59. Merry to Hawkesbury, Mar. 1, 1804, no. 19, FO 5/41.

60. Irving Brant in *James Madison: Secretary of State, 1800-1809* (pp. 170-71), holds that the United States rejected Article V of the King-Hawkesbury Convention of 1803 because Merry maintained that the convention was designed to give the British access to the Mississippi. This view hardly seems justified, since American misgivings had arisen before Merry had discussed the matter with Madison. See also Bradford Perkins, *The First Rapprochement*, p. 214, n. 30.

61. Hawkesbury to Merry, Sept. 16, 1803, no. 3 in Mayo, ed., *Instructions to the British Ministers*, p. 200.

62. Hawkesbury to Merry, Sept. 16, 1803, no. 2, ibid., p. 199.

63. Merry to Hawkesbury, Dec. 6, 1803, no. 2, FO 5/41.

64. Merry to Hawkesbury, Mar. 13, 1804, no. 23, FO 5/41.

65. Merry to Hawkesbury, Mar. 31, 1804, separate, FO 5/41.

66. Merry to Hammond, Oct. 1, 1804, private, FO 5/42.

67. Merry to Harrowby, Mar. 4, 1805, no. 10, FO 5/45.

68. Merry to Mulgrave, June 2, 1805, no. 25, FO 5/45.

69. Merry to Mulgrave, Sept. 2, 1805, no. 37, FO 5/45.

70. Merry to Mulgrave, Nov. 3, 1805, no. 45, FO 5/45.

71. John Armstrong to Madison, Sept. 10, 1805, Despatches from United States Ministers to France, vol. 10, SDR.

72. Merry to Mulgrave, Feb. 1, 1806, no. 6, FO 5/48.

73. Merry to Mulgrave, Mar. 19, 1806, no. 15, FO 5/48.

74. Senate Journal, Jan. 22, 1806, *Journal of the Senate of the United States of America, 1805-1811*, p. 26.

75. James Monroe to Madison, Oct. 18, 1805, Despatches from United States Ministers to Great Britain, vol. 12, SDR.

76. Merry to Mulgrave, March 19, 1806, no. 15, FO 5/48.

77. Ibid.

78. Merry to Fox, June 29, 1806, no. 34, FO 5/49.

79. Merry to Fox, Aug. 3, 1806, no. 38, FO 5/49.

80. Merry to Fox, Nov. 2, 1806, no. 51, FO 5/49.

81. *The Enquirer* (Richmond), Aug. 15, 1804; Merry to Fox, Aug. 31, 1806, no. 42, FO 5/49.

82. Merry to Hawkesbury, Mar. 31, 1804, no. 25, FO 5/41.

83. Merry to Fox, Nov. 2, 1806, no. 51, FO 5/49.

Chapter VI. Plots of Disunion

1. Henry Adams, *History of the United States during the Administrations of Thomas Jefferson and James Madison,* 2:391.

2. Dumas Malone, *Jefferson the President: First Term, 1801–1805,* p. 406.

3. Merrill D. Peterson, *Thomas Jefferson and the New Nation,* p. 794.

4. Nathan Schachner, *Aaron Burr,* p. 286.

5. Anthony Merry to Lord Hawkesbury, Mar. 1, 1804, no. 19, FO 5/41.

6. Merry to Hawkesbury, May 7, 1804, no. 32, FO 5/41. The "public suggestion" of an "individual of New England" cannot be identified.

7. Thomas Robson Hay, "Charles Williamson and the Burr Conspiracy," pp. 179–80.

8. Hawkesbury to Merry, Feb. 3, 1804, separate, in Bernard Mayo, ed., *Instructions to the British Ministers to the United States, 1791–1812,* p. 203.

9. Merry to Lord Harrowby, Aug. 6, 1804, no. 44, FO 5/42.

10. Merry to Hawkesbury, Mar. 13, 1804, No. 23, FO 5/41.

11. Thomas Perkins Abernethy, *The South in the New Nation, 1789–1819,* p. 332.

12. Merry to Harrowby, Mar. 29, 1805, no. 15, FO 5/45.

13. Sir Augustus John Foster, *Jeffersonian America,* pp. 281–82.

14. Richard Beale Davis, "Introduction" to Foster, *Jeffersonian America,* p. ix.

15. Merry to Harrowby, Mar. 29, 1805, no. 15, FO 5/45.

16. Merry to Lord Mulgrave, Apr. 29, 1805, no. 22, FO 5/45.

17. Adams, *History of the United States,* 2:403.

18. *Gazette of the United States* (Philadelphia), Aug. 2, 1805.

19. Merry to Mulgrave, Aug. 4, 1805, no. 34, FO 5/45.

20. Adams, *History of the United States,* 3:226.

21. Merry to Mulgrave, Nov. 25, 1805, no. 48, FO 5/45.

22. Thomas Perkins Abernethy, *The Burr Conspiracy,* p. 38.

23. James Madison to John Armstrong, May 27, 1807, in Madison, *The Writings of James Madison,* 7:446–49.

24. Madison, "Substance of a Communication made on the 23rd day of January, 1807, by Doctor Bollman to the President," in Madison, *Letters and Other Writings of James Madison,* 2:393–401.

25. Walter Flavius McCaleb, *The Aaron Burr Conspiracy and a New Light on Aaron Burr,* pp. 42–44, 65, 66, 299; Hay, "Charles Williamson and the Burr Conspiracy," p. 207.

26. Capt. John Poo Beresford, Memorandum, Dec. 13, [1806,] in Beresford-Peirse Archive, North Riding Record Office, County Hall, Northallerton.

27. McCaleb, *The Aaron Burr Conspiracy,* p. 64.

28. Adams, *History of the United States,* 3:250.

29. Abernethy, *The Burr Conspiracy,* p. 46.

30. Isaac J. Cox, "Hispanic Phase of the Burr Conspiracy," p. 153.

31. Abernethy, *The Burr Conspiracy,* pp. 59, 149.

32. Merry to Charles James Fox, Nov. 2, 1806, no. 52, FO 5/49.

33. Merry to Fox, Nov. 2, 1806, nos. 51, 52, FO 5/49.

34. David M. Erskine to Fox, Dec. 4, 1806, no. 2, FO 5/52.

35. Capt. Beresford, Memorandum, Dec. 13, [1806,] in Beresford-Peirse Archive.

36. Abernethy, *The Burr Conspiracy*, p. 37.

37. Yrujo to Cevallos, Dec. 5, 1805, as quoted in Adams, *History of the United States*, 3:234–35.

38. Stanley Lane-Pool, *Life of the Right Hon. Stratford Canning, Viscout Stratford de Redcliffe*, 1:30–32; Merry to George Jackson, Oct. 20, 1808, in *Diaries and Letters of Sir George Jackson*, 2:286–88.

39. Aaron Burr to Jeremy Bentham, Oct. 1 and 4, 1808, in *The Private Journals of Aaron Burr during his Residence of Four Years in Europe with Selections from His Correspondence*, 1:60–61, 66.

40. J. Leitch Wright, Jr., *Anglo-Spanish Rivalry in North America*, p. 166.

41. Merry to Burr, Nov. 6, 1808, in *Memoirs of Aaron Burr with Miscellaneous Selections from His Correspondence*, 2:413.

42. Schachner, *Aaron Burr*, p. 449.

Chapter VII. The End of the American Mission and Later Career

1. James Madison to Thomas Jefferson, Aug. 28, 1804, Thomas Jefferson Papers, LC.

2. Timothy Pickering to Robert Liston, Mar. 19, 1804, Timothy Pickering Papers, Massachusetts Historical Society, Boston.

3. Anthony Merry to Madison, Aug. 31, 1804, Notes from the British Legation, vol. 3, SDR.

4. Pickering to Timothy Williams, Nov. 16, 1807, Pickering Papers.

5. William Plumer, Memorandum, Mar. 11, 1806, in Plumer, *Memorandum of Proceedings in the United States Senate, 1803–1807*, p. 448.

6. Thomas Jefferson to James Maury, Apr. 25, 1812, in Jefferson, *The Writings of Thomas Jefferson* (Ford ed.), 9:348–51.

7. Augustus John Foster to Lady Elizabeth Foster, May 3, 1806. Augustus John Foster Papers, LC.

8. Merry to Lord Hawkesbury, Dec. 6, 1803, no. 1, FO 5/41.

9. Foster to Lady Elizabeth Foster, Sept. 22, 1805, Foster Papers.

10. Dorothy Margaret Stuart, *Dearest Bess*, p. 135.

11. Charles James Fox to Merry, Mar. 7, 1806, no. 1, in Bernard Mayo, ed., *Instructions to the British Ministers to the United States, 1791–1812*, p. 220.

12. Fox to the king, Mar. 6, 1806, in *The Later Correspondence of George III*, 4:405.

13. Thomas Erskine to Lord Grenville, May 22, 1806, in Papers of Lord Grenville in Historical Manuscripts Commission, *Reports on the Manuscripts of J. B. Fortescue Esq., Preserved at Dropmore*, 8:152.

14. Lord Colchester, Diary, Apr. 20, 1806, in *Diaries and Correspondence of Charles Abbot, Lord Colchester*, 2:51.

15. Merry to Madison, May 13, 1806, Notes from the British Legation, vol. 3, SDR.

16. Elizabeth Merry to Manasseh Cutler, May 17, 1806, in Cutler, *Life, Journals, and Correspondence*, 2:183.

17. Merry to Fox, June 1, 1806, private, FO 5/49.

18. Ibid.

19. Sir Francis Vincent to Merry, Aug. 8, 1806, separate, in Mayo, ed., *Instructions to the British Ministers*, p. 224.

20. Foster to Lady Elizabeth Foster, July 20, 1806, Foster Papers.

21. Foster to Lady Elizabeth Foster, Oct. 28, 1806, Foster Papers; Merry to Vincent, Nov. 2, 1806, private, FO 5/49.

22. S. T. Bindoff et al., *British Diplomatic Representatives, 1789–1852*, p. 185.

23. *National Intelligencer* (Washington, D.C.), Nov. 10, 1806.

24. Madison to James Monroe, Nov. 28, 1806, William Cabell Rives Papers, LC.

25. Merry to Madison, Nov. 29, 1806, Notes from the British Legation, vol. 3, State Department Records; Merry to Fox, Jan. 17, 1807, FO 5/55.

26. *Norfolk (Va.) Gazette*, Dec. 19, 1806; Merry to Fox, Jan. 17, 1807, FO 5/55.

27. Thomas Barclay to Adm. George C. Berkeley, Nov. 17, 1806, in Barclay, *Selections from the Correspondence of Thomas Barclay*, pp. 249–50; Foster to Lady Elizabeth Foster, Nov. 27 and Dec. 7, 1806, Foster Papers.

28. Quoted in Beckles Willson, *Friendly Relations*, p. 54.

29. Foster to Lady Elizabeth Foster, June 27, 1807, Foster Papers.

30. Merry to Fox, Jan. 17, 1807, FO 5/55.

31. Bindoff et al., *British Diplomatic Representatives*, pp. 43–44.

32. George Canning to the king, Sept. 27, 1807, in *The Later Correspondence of George III*, 4:631–32.

33. Lord Malmesbury Diaries, n.d., [1807], *Diaries and Correspondence of James Harris, First Earl*, 4:399.

34. Stanley Lane-Pool, *Life of the Right Hon. Stratford Canning, Viscount Stratford de Redcliffe*, pp. 30–32.

35. Merry to George Jackson, Oct. 20, 1808, in Jackson, *Diaries and Letters of Sir George Jackson*, 2:286–88.

36. Bindoff, et al., *British Diplomatic Representatives*, p. 151.

37. George Canning to the king, Dec. 22, 1808, in *The Later Correspondence of George III*, 5:161.

38. George Jackson, Diary, Dec. 16, 1809, in Jackson, *The Bath Archives*, 1:317–21.

39. William White, *History, Gazetteer, and Directory of Suffolk*, pp. 543–44.

40. John Burke, *Encyclopaedia of Heraldry, or General Armory of England, Scotland, and Ireland* entries alphabetically arranged under surname—see Merry; Sir George Jackson, Diary, Jan. 23 and 29, 1812, in Jackson, *The Bath Archives*, 1:317–21.

41. Will of Elizabeth Merry, May 21, 1817, proved June 5, 1824, Probate Registry, Somerset House, London.

42. Will of Anthony Merry, May 29, 1832, proved July 21, 1835, Probate Registry, Somerset House, London. Anthony Merry paid Gilbert Stuard $200 for painting this portrait (Charles Merrill Mount, *Gilbert Stuart*, p. 269). The Leathes family subsequently sold the portrait, which is reproduced in Lawrence Park, *Gilbert Stuart* (4:330); Don José Lazaro of Madrid was the last known owner, in 1926. Merry's portrait, also painted by Gilbert Stuart in 1805 (Park, 2:522–23), was in the possession of Dr. Sydney R. Merry of London in 1921 (Sydney R. Merry to John Franklin Jameson, Aug. 31, 1921, John Franklin Jameson Papers, LC). The present whereabouts of Merry's portrait is unknown, but it is reproduced in Irving Brant's *James Madison: Secretary of State, 1800–1809*, opposite p. 97, from a glass negative made for John Franklin Jameson and now in the Jameson Papers (John Franklin Jameson to W. E. Gray, Sept. 23, 1921, Jameson Papers). In my book the portrait of Anthony Merry (frontispiece) is reproduced from the Jameson negative and that of Elizabeth Merry (p. 11) is reproduced from the plate in Park.

43. Gerald H. Rendall, *Dedham Described and Deciphered*, p. 49. Anthony Merry's "Dedham House" was pulled down many years ago; the present "Dedham House" in the village has no connection with Merry or the earlier house.

44. Gerald H. Rendall to Jameson, Aug. 28, 1921, Jameson Papers.

45. Will of Anthony Merry, May 29, 1832, Probate Registry.

46. Codicil to the Will of Anthony Merry, Jan. 23, 1835, Probate Registry.

Bibliography

I. Manuscripts

British Museum, Department of Manuscripts, London.
  Osborne Papers, Additional Manuscript 28062
Guildhall Library, London.
  Parish Register of St. Laurence Pountney, Baptisms, 1740–1812, Manuscript 7667
Her Majesty's Public Record Office, London.
  Admiralty Papers
    Admirals' Despatches from the North American Station, Adm. 1/vols. 495, 496
    Captains' Letters, Adm. 1/vol. 1582
    Secretary's Letters to Commanders-in-Chief at Stations Abroad, Adm. 2/vol. 931
  Foreign Office Papers
    General Correspondence, FO 5/vols. 38, 41, 42, 43, 44, 45, 48, 49, 52, 55
    Francis James Jackson Papers, FO 353/vol. 76
    Stratford Canning Papers, FO 352/vol. 8
Library of Congress, Division of Manuscripts, Washington.
  Augustus John Foster Papers
  John Franklin Jameson Papers
  Thomas Jefferson Papers
  James Madison Papers
  James Monroe Papers
  William Cabell Rives Papers
  Transcripts from Archives des Affaires Etrangères, Correspondence Politique, Etats-Unis
Massachusetts Historical Society, Boston.
  Thomas Jefferson Papers
  Timothy Pickering Papers
National Library of Scotland, Edinburgh.
  Sir Robert Liston Papers
New-York Historical Society, New York.
  Rufus King Papers
North Riding Record Office, County Hall, Northallerton.
  Beresford-Peirse Archive

Probate Registry, Somerset House, London.
  Will of Anthony Merry, May 29, 1832
  Codicil to the Will of Anthony Merry, January 23, 1835
  Will of Elizabeth Merry, May 21, 1817
United States National Archives, Washington.
  State Department Records
    Despatches from the United States Ministers to France, vol. 10
    Despatches from the United States Ministers to Great Britain, vol. 12
    Notes from the British Legation, vol. 3

II. Contemporary Newspapers and Periodicals

Aurora. 1803–4 (Philadelphia).
Cobbett's Annual Register. 1803 (London).
Cobbett's Weekly Political Register. 1804 (London).
The Enquirer. 1806 (Richmond, Va.).
Gazette of the United States. 1804–5 (Philadelphia).
Gentleman's Magazine. 1783–1803 (London).
National Intelligencer. 1806 (Washington).
Norfolk Gazette. 1806 (Norfolk, Va.)   .
The Port Folio. vol. 4, 1804 (Philadelphia).

II. Government Documents

*American State Papers: Document, Legislative and Executive of the Congress of the
  United States, Selected and Edited under the Authority of Congress.* 38 vols.
  Washington, D.C., 1832–61.
*Annals of Congress: Debates and Proceedings, First Congress, First Session,
  March 3, 1789, to Eighteenth Congress, First Session, May 27, 1824.* 42 vols.
  Washington, D.C., 1834–56.
Burrell, Sir William. *Reports of Cases Determined by the High Court of Admiralty.*
  Edited by Reginald G. Marsden. London, 1885.
Journal of the Senate of the United States of America, 1805–11. Washington,
  D.C., 1821.
London Directory. 1780.
Mayo, Bernard, ed. *Instructions to the British Ministers to the United States,
  1791–1812.* American Historical Association Annual Report for 1936,
  vol. 3. Washington, D.C., 1941.

Richardson, James D., ed. *A Compilation of the Messages and Papers of the Presidents, 1789–1897.* 10 vols. Washington, D.C., 1897–1900.

Savage, Carlton, ed. *Policy of the United States Toward Maritime Commerce in War.* 2 vols. Washington, D.C., 1934.

United States Statutes at Large from the Organization of the Government in 1789 to March 3, 1845. 8 vols. Boston, 1845–51.

IV. Writings of Contemporaries

Barclay, Thomas. *Selections from the Correspondence of Thomas Barclay.* Edited by George L. Rives. New York, 1894.

Battle, Kemp P., ed. *"Letters of Nathaniel Macon, John Steele, and William Barry Grove."* James Sprunt Historical Monographs, vol. 3 Chapel Hill, N.C., 1902.

Biddle, Nicholas. "Private Journal." Edited by Edward Biddle. In *Pennsylvania Magazine of History and Biography*, 55 (1931):208–24.

Brougham, Henry, Lord. *Life and Times of Henry, Lord Brougham.* 3 vols. London, 1871.

Burney, Fanny (Madame D'Arblay). *The Journals and Letters of Fanny Burney (Madame D'Arblay).* Edited by Joyce Hemlow. 6 vols. Oxford, 1972–75.

Burr, Aaron, *Memoirs of Aaron Burr with Miscellaneous Selections from His Correspondence.* Edited by Matthew L. Davis. 2 vols. New York, 1855.

_____. *The Private Journals of Aaron Burr during His Residence of Four Years in Europe with Selections from His Correspondence.* Edited by Matthew L. Davis. 2 vols. New York, 1838.

Colchester, Lord. *The Diary and Correspondence of Charles Abbot, Lord Colchester.* Edited by Charles, Lord Colchester [his son]. 3 vols. London, 1861.

Cornwallis, Charles, First Marquis. *Correspondence.* Edited by Charles Ross. 3 vols. London, 1859.

Cutler, Manasseh. *Life, Journals, and Correspondence.* Edited by William P. and Julia P. Cutler. 2 vols. Cincinnati, 1888.

Foster, Sir Augustus John. *Jeffersonian America: Notes on the United States of America Collected in the Years 1805–6–7 and 11–12 By Sir Augustus John Foster, Bart.* Edited with an introduction by Richard Beale Davis. San Marino, Calif., 1954.

George III. *The Later Correspondence of George III.* Edited by A. Aspinall. 5 vols. Cambridge, 1966–70.

Glenbervie, Sylvester Douglas, Lord. *The Diaries of Sylvester Douglas, Lord Glenbervie.* Edited by Francis Bickley. 2 vols. London, 1928.

Granville, Granville Leveson-Gower, Earl. *Private Correspondence, 1781–1821*. Edited by Countess Granville. 2 vols. London, 1916.

Grenville, William Wyndham, First Baron. Papers of Lord Grenville in Historical Manuscripts Commission, *Report on the Manuscripts of J. B. Fortescue, Esq., Preserved at Dropmore*. Edited by Walter Fitzpatrick and Francis Bickley. 10 vols. London, 1892–1927.

Jackson, Sir George. *The Bath Archives: A Further Selection from the Diaries and Letters of Sir George Jackson from 1809 to 1816*. Edited by Lady Jackson. 2 vols. London, 1873.

_____. *Diaries and Letters of Sir George Jackson from the Peace of Amiens to the Battle of Talavera*. Edited by Lady Jackson. 2 vols. London, 1872.

Jefferson, Thomas. *The Writings of Thomas Jefferson*. Edited by Paul Leicester Ford. 10 vols. New York, 1892–99.

_____. *The Writings of Thomas Jefferson*. Edited by Andrew A. Lipscomb and Albert E. Bergh. 20 vols. Washington, D.C., 1803.

King, Rufus. *Life and Correspondence of Rufus King*. Edited by Charles R. King. 6 vols. New York, 1894–99.

Madison, James. *Letters and Other Writings of James Madison, Fourth President of the United States, Published by Order of Congress*. 4 vols. Philadelphia, 1865.

_____. *The Writings of James Madison*. Edited by Gaillard Hunt. 9 vols. New York, 1900–1910.

Malmesbury, James Harris, Earl of. *Diaries and Correspondence of James Harris, First Earl*. Edited by the Third Earl. 4 vols. London, 1844.

Monroe, James. *The Writings of James Monroe*. Edited by Stanislaus Murray Hamilton. 7 vols. New York, 1898–1903.

Moore, Thomas. *Memoirs, Journal, and Correspondence*. Edited by Lord John Russell. 8 vols. London, 1853–56.

Paget, Sir Arthur. *Diplomatic and Other Correspondence*. Edited by Sir Augustus B. Paget. 2 vols. London, 1896.

Plumer, William. *Memorandum of Proceedings in the United States Senate, 1803–1807*. Edited by Everett S. Brown. New York, 1923.

Smith, Margaret Bayard. *The First Forty Years of Washington Society*. Edited by Gaillard Hunt. New York, 1906.

Taggart, Samuel. "Letters of Samuel Taggart, Representative in Congress, 1803–1814." Introduction by George H. Haynes. In *Proceedings of the American Antiquarian Society*, vol. 33 (1923), pt. 1 (1803–7), pp. 113–226.

Temple, William Johnston. *Diaries of William Johnston Temple, 1780–1796*. Edited, with a memoir, by Lewis Bettany. Oxford, 1929.

V. Secondary Works and Articles

Abernethy, Thomas Perkins. *The Burr Conspiracy.* New York, 1954.

————. *The South in the New Nation, 1789–1819.* Baton Rouge, La.; 1961.

Adams, Henry. *History of the United States during the Administrations of Thomas Jefferson and James Madison.* 9 vols. New York, 1889–91.

Alger, John B. *Napoleon's British Visitors and Captives, 1801–1815.* New York, 1904.

Ammon, Harry. *James Monroe: The Quest for National Identity.* New York, 1971.

Bindoff, S. T., E. F. Malcolm Smith, and C. K. Webster. *British Diplomatic. Representatives, 1789–1852.* London, 1934.

Bowers, Claude G. *Jefferson in Power.* Boston, 1936.

Brant, Irving. *James Madison: Secretary of State, 1800–1809.* Indianapolis, 1953.

Burke, John. *Encyclopaedia of Heraldry, or General Armory of England, Scotland, and Ireland.* London, 1847.

Campbell, John, Baron. *Lives of the Lord Chancellors and Keepers of the Great Seal of England.* 10 vols. London, 1868.

Channing, Edward. *The Jeffersonian System.* New York, 1906.

Clark, Allen Culling. *Life and Letters of Dolly Madison.* Washington, D.C., 1914.

Cox, Isaac J. "Hispanic-American Phases of the Burr Conspiracy." *Hispanic-American Historical Review* 12 (1932): 145–72.

————. *The West Florida Controversy, 1798–1818.* Baltimore, 1918.

Eberlain, Harold Donaldson, and Cortlandt Van Dyke Hubbard. *Historic Houses of George-Town & Washington City.* Richmond, 1958.

Hay, Thomas Robson. "Charles Williamson and the Burr Conspiracy." *Journal of Southern History* 2 (1936):175–210.

Holt, W. Stull. *Treaties Defeated by the Senate.* Baltimore, 1933.

Horn, D. B. *The British Diplomatic Service, 1689–1789.* Oxford, 1961.

Johnston, Albert Richard. *The Parish Church of St. Mary, Dedham.* London, 1966.

Jones, Howard Mumford. *The Harp That Once—: A Chronicle of the Life of Thomas Moore.* New York, 1937.

Ketcham, Ralph. *James Madison, A Biography.* New York, 1971.

Lane-Pool, Stanley. *Life of the Right Hon. Stratford Canning, Viscount Stratford de Redcliffe.* 2 vols. London, 1888.

Larus, Joel. "Pell Mell Along the Potomac." *William and Mary Quarterly,* 3rd ser. 17 (1960):349–57.

McCaleb, Walter Flavius. *The Aaron Burr Conspiracy and a New Light on Aaron Burr.* New York, 1966.

Malone, Dumas. *Jefferson the President: First Term, 1801–1805.* Boston, 1970.

————. *Jefferson the President: Second Term, 1805–1809.* Boston, 1974.

Manning, William R. "The Nootka Sound Controversy." In American Historical Association, *Annual Report for 1904,* pp. 279–478. Washington, D.C., 1905.

Mount, Charles Merrill. *Gilbert Stuart: A Biography.* New York, 1964.

Neel, Joanne Loewe. *Phineas Bond: A Study in Anglo-American Relations, 1786–1812.* Philadelphia, 1968.

Osborne, John W. *William Cobbett: His Thought and Times.* New Brunswick, N.J., 1966.

Park, Lawrence. *Gilbert Stuart: An Illustrated Descriptive List of His Works Compiled by Lawrence Park and An Account of His Life by John Hill Morgan and An Appreciation by Royal Cortissoz.* 4 vols. New York, 1926.

Perkins, Bradford. *The First Rapprochement: England and the United States, 1795–1805.* Philadelphia, 1955.

————. *Prologue to War: England and the United States, 1805–1812.* Berkeley, Calif., 1963.

Peterson, Merrill D. *Thomas Jefferson and the New Nation.* New York, 1970.

Quincy, Edmund. *Life of Josiah Quincy.* Boston, 1867.

Randall, Henry S. *Life of Thomas Jefferson.* 3 vols. New York, 1858.

Rendall, Gerald H. *Dedham Described and Deciphered.* Colchester, Eng., 1937.

Rose, John Holland. *Life of William Pitt.* 2 vols. London, 1923.

Schachner, Nathan. *Aaron Burr, A Biography.* New York, 1937.

Seton-Watson, Robert W. *Britain in Europe.* Cambridge, 1937.

Smelser, Marshall. *The Democratic Republic, 1801–1815.* New York, 1968.

Steel, Anthony. "Anthony Merry and the Anglo-American Dispute about Impressment, 1803–1806." *Cambridge Historical Journal* 9 (1949): 331–51.

Stuart, Dorothy M. *Dearest Bess: The Life and Times of Lady Elizabeth Foster, afterwards Duchess of Devonshire, from Her Unpublished Journals and Correspondence.* London, 1955.

Watson, Winslow Marston. *In Memoriam: Benjamin Ogle Tayloe.* Washington, D.C., 1872.

White, William. *History, Gazetteer, and Directory of Suffolk.* Sheffield, Eng., 1855.

Willson, Beckles. *Friendly Relations: A Narrative of Britain's Ministers and Ambassadors to America, 1791–1930.* London, 1934.

Wright, J. Leitch, Jr. *Anglo-Spanish Rivalry in North America.* Athens, Ga., 1971.

————. *Britain and the American Frontier, 1783–1815.* Athens, Ga., 1975.

Yonge, Charles Duke. *The Life and Administration of Robert Banks, Second Earl of Liverpool, K. G., Late First Lord of the Treasury, Compiled from Original Documents.* 3 vols. London, 1868.

Zimmerman, James Fulton. *Impressment of American Seamen.* New York, 1925.

Index